IMAGES
*of America*

# SURFING IN
# SAN DIEGO

**ON THE COVER:** "This is a shot of the Coronado Surf Club when they gathered at North Beach in 1963. The tide pool in the foreground was absolutely still and glassy while I was preparing to shoot, and I knew I only had a few minutes. My first attempt turned out too dark, and this was my second photograph. Then the wind blew across and ruined any other opportunities I might have had. I think it's one of my signature photos," said Tom Keck, describing his photograph.

IMAGES
*of America*

# SURFING IN
# SAN DIEGO

John C. Elwell, Jane Schmauss, and
the California Surf Museum

ARCADIA
PUBLISHING

Published by Arcadia Publishing
Charleston, South Carolina

Library of Congress Catalog Card Number: 2007920168

For all general information contact Arcadia Publishing at:
Telephone 843-853-2070
Fax 843-853-0044
E-mail sales@arcadiapublishing.com
For customer service and orders:
Toll-Free 1-888-313-2665

Visit us on the Internet at www.arcadiapublishing.com

*This book is dedicated to all San Diegans who embrace the surfing lifestyle. This is their story.*

# CONTENTS

# ACKNOWLEDGMENTS

Many of the photographs that appear in this book come from the archives of the California Surf Museum (CSM), unless otherwise noted, and CSM feels it has been a privilege to be a part of this production. Dozens of people helped with the research and compilation of the data, and we are very grateful for their participation.

The team from CSM did a fantastic job. John Elwell, Jack "Woody" Ekstrom, Tom Keck, and Lee Louis supplied many of the images from their sizable collections and provided insights for the accompanying captions. CSM's associate director, Ryan A. Smith, tightened things editorially and helped keep the project on track. Behind-the-scenes workers Barbara Allen, Eric Chen, Nick Schmiege, Todd Quinn, Tom Glenn, and Tara Lee Torburn brought their considerable skills to the task. A special thank you must also be extended to the Cardiff Library and its staff for providing the workspace where we met and planned this book.

Our deepest gratitude goes to the following individuals for generously sharing their personal collections with us: LeRoy Grannis, Emil Sigler, Richard Dowdy, Richard James, Jim "Mouse" Robb, Tani Church Bell, Shirley Richards, John Oakley, Bill "Hadji" Hein, Mike "Electric Duck" Richardson, Laura Kaye, Evelyn Largent, Fred Ashley, Diana Brummett, Glen McInery, Terry Curren, Dr. Kenneth Haygood, Michael Dormer, L. J. Richards, Cramer Jackson, Marsh Malcolm, Carl Knox, Jack Lounsberry, Robert "Black Mac" McClendon, Ken Woodward, Mike Burner, Bud Caldwell, Tommy Lewis, Don Craig, and the families of Faye Baird Fraser, Ralph Noisat, and Hank Algert. We are also grateful for the contributions of Doug Tico, Ron McCarver, Jens Morrison, Kit Horn, Carl Miller, Tillman Eakes, Greg Hogan, Tom Morey, Eddy Hodge, Lollie Taylor, Jean Korbacher, Gerry Kirk, Carl Ekstrom, Hans Newman, Steve Clark, Kimball Daun, Remington Jackson, Tom Cozens, Ben Siegfried, Cher Threinen-Pendarvis, Patti Magee, Bobby "Challenger" Thomas, and David Aguirre.

Many thanks to the local historical agencies for sharing their bounty with us, namely the San Dieguito Heritage Museum (SDHM), San Diego Historical Society (SDHS), La Jolla Historical Society (LJHS), and Del Mar Historical Society (DMHS). We used the following publications for basic research and fact-checking: *The Encyclopedia of Surfing* by Matt Warshaw, *Girl in the Curl* by Andrea Gabbard, and "90 Years of Curl" by Jeannette DeWyze, from the *San Diego Weekly Reader*, December 14, 2006.

# INTRODUCTION

Surfing is what we do when we ride a wave in the ocean. There is an energy generated in this liaison of man and sea that creates a "stoke" that is like no other. Whether we body surf or board surf, we experience the joy of surfing. San Diego County possesses nearly 75 miles of Pacific Ocean coastline that offers an enviable assortment of sandy beaches, reef breaks, rocky shores, coves, cliffs, peninsulas, and point breaks. Its shoreline receives swells from Pacific storms that come from many directions and cause wave formations of varying intensities. The characteristics of these waves are changed on our beaches and reefs and thus provide very consistent, moderate-to-excellent surfing conditions. Surfing and San Diego have gone hand in hand since the beginning of the last century, and this is the story we wish to tell.

Surfing first arrived in Southern California in 1907 when Hawaiian-born George Freeth was hired to do a series of surfing and other water sports demonstrations in the Redondo Beach area. This athletic man who "walked on water" with such style and ease entertained vast numbers of beachgoers. Soon after these demonstrations, the locals enthusiastically took to the ocean, crafting boards of their own and imitating his considerable skills.

Ralph Noisat was already a San Diego surfer when George Freeth arrived in town in 1915. Duke Kahanamoku, a native Hawaiian known as the "Father of Modern Surfing," visited in 1916, and lifeguard Charlie Wright made a copy of Duke's board that was used time and again in Old Mission Beach. Many folks at the beach were already enjoying aquaplaning, skimboarding, and freeboarding, and when Emil Sigler arrived on the scene in 1928, his stand-up surfing style renewed interest in yet another form of the sport. Surfing blossomed in the 1930s, and San Diegans were discovering a veritable banquet of surfing sites between San Onofre and Imperial Beach.

The impact of surfing on San Diego has been huge, and it now extends into the mainstream of American culture. But that was not always the case. Many years ago, a small tribe of dedicated watermen hauled huge planks into the water and surfed without wet suits or leashes. What had been the signature sport for a select few has gradually become the recreational pastime of thousands, and this is a first attempt to put that story in book form. Dozens of residents of San Diego County stepped forward to offer cherished photographs and anecdotes of their surfing experiences of long ago. In true "talking story" tradition, we accepted these colorful tales and wove them into the captions where we could. Their photographs and recollections, we sincerely hope, are the main attractions of this simple book.

Come along with the California Surf Museum as we take a pictorial journey of surfing in San Diego, from the mid-1900s to the mid-1960s. Told through the power of photographs, the story of having fun in the ocean is paramount. Depicted are strong, healthy, vibrant, happy, and handsome athletes and characters that spent much of their free time devoted to the surfing lifestyle. We hope you enjoy the adventure back in time, to an earlier, less crowded, and classic San Diego.

The philosophy of *Surfing in San Diego* can be best described by a quote from 1930s pioneer surfer Kimball Daun: "If we weren't out surfing, we were thinking about it. That's who we were."

# One

# THE EARLY YEARS

To date, San Diego's earliest surf history has gone largely undocumented. At two different times, fire destroyed local newspaper collections, and a great deal of important information has been lost. The California Surf Museum has gone back in time and gathered data from many individuals in order to piece together this fascinating story. Lifeguard Charlie Wright was one of the most visible fellows to step on a surfboard in San Diego. This photograph appeared in the *San Diego Sun* on September 5, 1925, and announced the first surfboard meet ever held. It reads: "Charlie Wright, life-guard and sponsor of a surfboard tournament in North Mission Beach Monday. Behind him is a board of the type to be considered regulation in the meet. It is 9 1/2 feet long, 3 inches thick, 2 feet wide, and weighs 100 pounds." The young child is Louisa Alline Taylor, according to the San Diego Historical Society archives. Four days later, a sports section article headline read: "Wright Wins Surf Contest—Ernest Judd Cops Second Prize in Breaker Riding Tournament." (Courtesy of SDHS.)

Duke Paoa Kahanamoku, a Hawaiian considered the "Father of Modern Surfing," made several excursions to San Diego. He was already an Olympic swimming gold medalist when he arrived in 1916 as the star attraction of "Hawaiian Week." Locals crowded the beaches for the events, where most spectators saw stand-up surfing for the first time. While in town, Duke and his good friend and swimming coach George Freeth surfed in Ocean Beach, and Duke, at one point, loaned his board to Charlie Wright. Duke returned to San Diego on several occasions thereafter and was named honorary chairman of the 1966 World Championships in Ocean Beach.

Members of the Cozens family are dressed for a day at the beach in Del Mar in 1915. These Encinitas-area pioneers enjoyed frequent beach outings in the summer months. Bert Cozens stands in the far back. (Courtesy of SDHM.)

Aquaplaning was a popular water sport at the beginning of the 20th century. One had to balance on a board that was attached by rope to a speeding boat, all while holding tightly to the towline. Pictured here around 1920, some hardy folks get some great exercise in the ocean waters off Coronado. (Courtesy of SDHM.)

Ralph Noisat, whose family settled in San Diego in 1910, was passionate about surfing. One of the state's first truly avid surfers, Ralph may have been among the first to test the waves in San Diego as well. Ralph's grandfather was an engineer at the Pioneer Sugar Mill on Maui and brought the lad a piece of exotic wood so he could build his own surfboard. In the mid-1900s, Ralph surfed the unspoiled California coast from San Diego to San Francisco and, later, as a naval officer, took this 7-foot, squaretail surfboard (seen here) with him everywhere.

Born on Oahu in 1883, George Freeth is credited as being the first man to bring surfboard riding to Southern California. In 1907, the accomplished swimmer, diver, and surfer was hired to thrill overflow crowds in Venice and Redondo Beach with his amazing exhibitions of "walking on water."

George Freeth, instrumental in setting up the California lifeguard system still used today, taught basic water-rescue techniques in San Diego. Freeth devised much of the rescue equipment (seen here) himself and was awarded a Congressional Gold Medal in 1908 after dramatically saving 11 Japanese fishermen during a violent winter storm.

In 1915, the San Diego Rowing Club lured Freeth to the area in order to coach their swimming team. For the record, a July 17, 1918, *San Diego Union* article recorded the following: "4000 beachgoers received a surprise and enjoyed a succession of thrills and healthy laughs yesterday when George Freeth, lifeguard, presented his unannounced surfboard 'dive.' Riding on the crest of the wave in the usual manner, Freeth suddenly leaped, clearing the board by at least 3 feet, turned a somersault, regained his balance on the board again, and completed his stunt with a dive." (Courtesy of SDHS.)

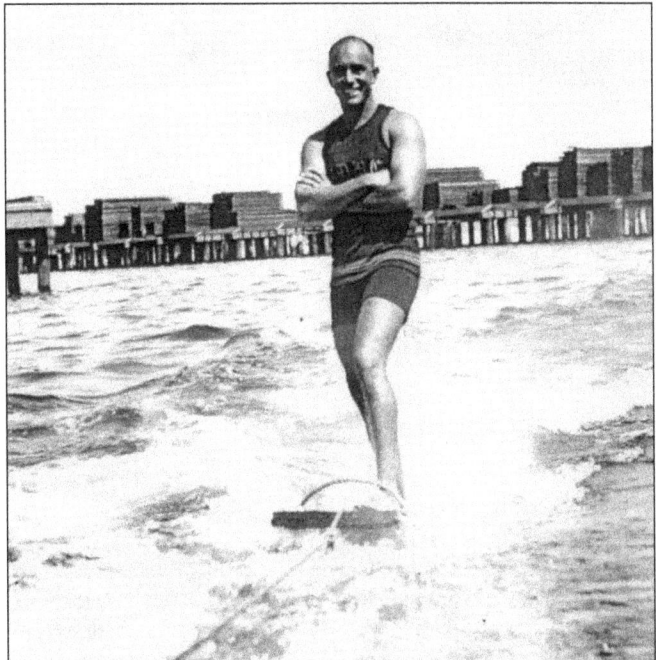

Sadly, this giant of an athlete and waterman was not strong enough to escape the grip of the deadly influenza epidemic that swept the nation during his time. A prominent obituary in the *San Diego Union* on Wednesday, April 9, 1919, reads, "In the death of George Douglas Freeth, his hundreds of friends here and elsewhere will mourn the loss of a true friend and a lovable character, while aquatic circles of the Pacific coast will lose one who held undisputed authority and knowledge of water sport. The direct cause of his demise being a severe attack of acute domination of the heart." (Courtesy of SDHS.)

Charlie Wright made this board, named "Iron Tip," by copying Duke Kahanamoku's plank when he visited San Diego in 1916, and Charlie generously loaned the board to anyone who had the strength and desire to get it into the ocean. According to Robert C. Baxley, "Charlie taught me, and many other local boys, to swim. He was a healthy, solid, kind man. . . . At one time he had been a stuntman in the movies so, to all the kids, he was a hero." (Courtesy of Faye Baird Fraser.)

Teenage distance swimmer Faye Baird Fraser carries a waterproof flare while being towed on Charlie Wright's surfboard. By all accounts, Charlie was a bit of a showman, and he and his partners put on a terrific program for New Year's Eve, 1925. (Courtesy of Faye Baird Fraser.)

Charlie Wright and Faye Baird Fraser perform a tandem routine in 1926. Faye often borrowed the sizable board to test her skills in the waves. She recalled: "On one of my very first solos, I caught a wave much too close to the pier and found myself barreling right through the pilings. Scared me to death! I later found out that that maneuver was called 'shooting the pier,' and only the most skilled surfers attempted it. Guess I was just lucky!" (Courtesy of Faye Baird Fraser.)

Faye Baird Fraser later remarked that, though it was a very cold winter night when they performed their New Year's Eve water stunts, she didn't feel the chill: "Sure, it was cold that night, but with hundreds of folks out on the beach and pier cheering us on, we didn't even notice. I went to the big dance at the ballroom afterwards." (Courtesy of Faye Baird Fraser.)

Originally from Arizona, Henry "Hank" Algert attended San Diego's Army-Navy Academy before, ultimately, graduating from San Diego High School. Hank became a surfer and freeboarder after he saw Duke Kahanamoku performing water stunts in Coronado in 1916. The two became acquainted when Duke needed a motorboat to put on an aquaplaning performance, and Hank offered his. In the 1920s, Hank started a freeboarding business, using his boat at La Jolla Cove, and made spending money by towing tourists along La Jolla Shores. (Courtesy of the Algert family.)

At a solid 5 feet 8 inches, Hank's strong physique was the result of several seasons of work with the local Portuguese fishermen hauling tuna into the boat, hour after hour. Here Hank is pictured standing at the foot of Devil's Slide, which was built by the railroad company in order to access La Jolla Cove's thriving tide pools. Behind him is his prized boat, which was dashed to pieces on the rocks the following winter. (Courtesy of the Algert family.)

Scott Palmer, who shaped the boards seen here, took this photograph of his daughters Erma and Bertha in 1924 at Old Mission Beach. The shorter, thinner boards were mostly used for bodyboarding and skimboarding, not stand-up surfing. (Courtesy of SDHS.)

Leaning against a dory at Old Mission Beach, Emil Sigler wears a regulation lifeguard suit from the late 1920s. Emil was a strong swimmer and an expert dory man. In the early 1930s, Emil and fellow guard Bill Rumsey borrowed a dory and rowed up the coast to Los Angeles. The waterlogged pair had no money once they landed, so they were granted permission to spend the night in a Hermosa Beach jail. The next day, they rowed to Catalina Island for a few days of fishing and camping. (Courtesy of Emil Sigler.)

17

As a youth in San Francisco, Emil Sigler was fascinated by two Hawaiian lifeguards from the Fleishhacker Plunge who took their wooden boards into the ocean during their off time. When Emil moved to San Diego in 1928, he systematically searched the beach towns for such boards, finally locating one at Charlie Wright's headquarters. Charlie gladly let Emil borrow it, and it was from this prototype that Emil crafted a few boards of his own. (Courtesy of Emil Sigler.)

After arriving in San Diego, Emil made his home at Old Mission Beach and immediately began taking pictures. An amateur photographer with a love of all things ocean, Emil captured the simple, carefree lifestyle of that time. A compilation of his work can be found in his recently published book, A Waterman's Eye. Here Emil captured the Old Mission Beach lifeguard crew in 1928. The men are wearing regulation swimsuits of that time, which kept their upper torsos covered while at the beach. (Courtesy of Emil Sigler.)

# Two

# SOUTH COUNTY

South County beaches include coastal territories from the Mexican border north to Coronado, with Imperial Beach and the Silver Strand highlighted in between. In this photograph, Chuck "Gunker" Quinn from Coronado brings his Bob Simmons surfboard to the Tijuana Sloughs in 1952. Gunker, a San Diego County lifeguard, relied on phone calls from Allan "Dempsey" Holder to alert him whenever giant surf was expected. When large northwest swells closed out the coast, big-wave surfers from all over received calls from Dempsey and then journeyed south to the Sloughs, California's first big-wave break. (Photograph by John Elwell.)

Pictured here in the late 1960s, Dempsey Holder rides a homemade knockoff of a Simmons surfboard in front of the Palm Street lifeguard station at Imperial Beach. Dempsey was one of the most respected big-wave surfers and watermen on the mainland's Pacific Coast. A natural leader and mentor to scores of youngsters, he was also an exceptional athlete who excelled at track and field, basketball, and golf. Dempsey was a veteran San Diego City lifeguard and, in 1939, became the first county lifeguard at Imperial Beach, where the Aquatic Center bears his name. These days, Dempsey Holder is considered a surfing legend, having pioneered the infamous Tijuana Sloughs, a deep reef stretching a mile offshore that produces some of the largest and longest waves in Southern California. (Courtesy of John Elwell.)

San Diego County lifeguard John Elwell stands in front of Dempsey Holder's lifeguard service truck at the Tijuana Sloughs on a cold, winter, big surf day in 1951. A Coronado native, John surfed all of San Diego's major wave-rich areas and, in the mid-1950s, was an integral part of the early migrations of Californian surfers to test Oahu's unconquered North Shore. (Courtesy of John Elwell.)

Four Simmons boards are pictured in the back of Dempsey Holder's service truck at Imperial Beach in 1952. Two years earlier, when Bob Simmons came to surf the area, he and his specially designed boards moved across the waves with such amazing speed that the locals immediately dubbed him the "Phantom Surfer." Here Chuck Quinn (left) and Tom Carlin prepare to drive south to the sloughs for some serious surf. (Courtesy of John Elwell.)

"Red" Richardson took this photograph of his son Mike surfing at the Tijuana Sloughs during a winter swell in 1962. Mike is wearing the top half of a diving wet suit called a "beavertail" because of the long flap that hung from the back and fastened to the front. (Courtesy of Mike Richardson.)

Jim Barber (left) and Sean Holder, son of Dempsey Holder, share a slide on an overhead wave at the outside shore break of the Tijuana Sloughs in 1965, captured by photographer Kim Dodds. Jim and Sean were among the group of South County gremmies (young surfers who tried to emulate the older surfers) in Imperial Beach at the time. (Courtesy of Mike Richardson.)

The Imperial Beach Pier was still under construction when this 1962 photograph was taken. Mike Richardson gets a fine left-hand ride on his custom Duane Brown semi-gun surfboard. (Photograph by Red Richardson; courtesy of Mike Richardson.)

Finding inventive ways to keep the surf stoke alive even when the waves went flat, Mike Richardson shoots a huge smile to his parents as they tow him aside the family's 14-foot, 75-horsepower ski boat. Here Mike hangs five just above the shallows on the bay side of the Silver Strand. (Courtesy of Mike Richardson.)

A solid summertime wave breaks at Coronado's North Beach as a low-flying seabird glides in front of the Point Loma peninsula. Coronado has produced a long list of respected surfers thanks to its unique beach waves. (Courtesy of John Elwell.)

Jim Renfro catches a shoulder-high left at North Beach in Coronado in the early 1960s. Due to its unique angle, North Beach provides fun summer surf for South County surfers. (Photograph by John Elwell.)

David Chalmers takes his dog Max out surfing with him. The pair surfed up and down the coast, and David even glued a piece of rubber on the tip of this board's nose so Max could get a good grip with his toenails. Seen here surfing Center Beach in Coronado, Max was only one of a number of dogs who were hooked on surfing in the San Diego area. (Photograph by Steve Ogles; courtesy of Mike Richardson.)

Tom Sanders crouches below the thin lip of a glassy North Beach right in this 1962 photograph taken by John Elwell. (Photograph by John Elwell.)

The Hotel Del Coronado provides a dramatic backdrop for an exciting canoe-jousting contest. During these impromptu events, each man would stand in his canoe and try to topple an opponent into the water using a long jousting stick that was covered with a ball on one end. (Courtesy of Terry Curren.)

Hobie Alter (third from right) and two Explorer Scouts look on as Mike Dobransky (left) explains the finer points of surf style to the Scoutmaster. Tom Keck took this photograph in 1964. (Courtesy of Tom Keck.)

On an overcast summer's day, participants cast their eyes seaward to watch the progress of a contest held at Coronado in the mid-1960s. The famous Hotel Del Coronado is seen in the background. (Photograph by John Elwell.)

Margie Manock catches a small wave on her 9-foot, 18-pound Bob Simmons surfboard in 1950. Margie was Coronado's first female surfer and one of the few women Simmons made a custom board for. (Photograph by John Elwell.)

27

"This get-together was held by the surf clubs of Coronado and Del Mar in an attempt to draw attention to the need to keep the local beaches clean," says photographer Tom Keck. "Held in 1964, I believe that this was one of the first environmental beach clean-ups ever held." (Photograph by Tom Keck.)

Two young surfers in Coronado, Dennis Downs (left) and Tom Moran, stop to examine a discarded case of dead chickens that was likely tossed overboard from a passing U.S. Navy ship in 1963. The Hotel Del Coronado can faintly be seen in the background. (Photograph by Tom Keck.)

These two photographs come from a classic scrapbook found at a swap meet and donated to the California Surf Museum. The scrapbook documents a lot of the social and business activities of a surf club called "The Outsiders," which seems to have been headquartered in National City around 1963. Eddy Hodge, coolly decked out in sunglasses and a Pendleton (the "surfer's choice") shirt, poses with three boards.

Gasper Galindo takes the wax off his board after a session at Imperial Beach. The Outsiders were a very social club and held activities ranging from dances and movies to clothing and toy drives for a Tijuana orphanage. On occasion, the club would test their surfing mettle in local competitions against teams from Windansea, Pacific Beach, and other coastal towns. Former Outsider Eddy Hodge recalled: "I knew I was in trouble when I faced Skip Frye, Corky Carroll, and Donald Takayama in my same heat. I was way out of my league! But, heck, we just surfed for fun anyway."

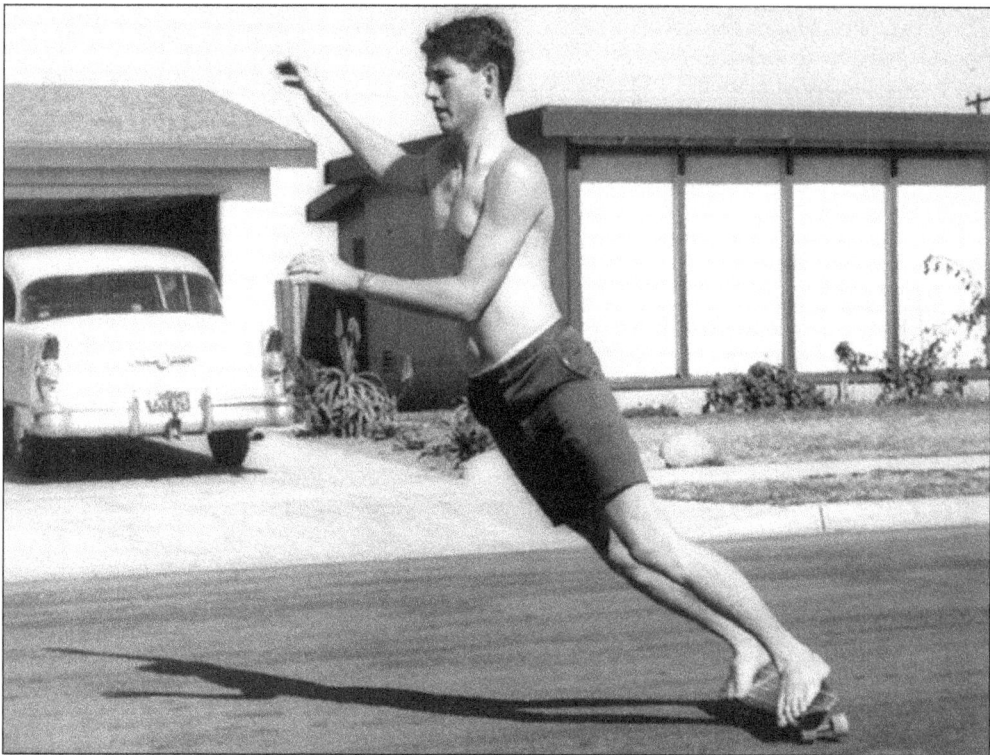

Mike Richardson shows classic style and balance on the brand-new Hobie skateboard his parents gave him for Christmas, 1963. Before the early 1960s, most youngsters were forced to construct their own skateboards from skate wheels and wood planks. (Courtesy of Mike Richardson.)

"That's me doing a headstand on a small surf day," recalls Mike Richardson. "Richard Joly shaped this beautiful five-stringer board for me when he worked for South Coast Surfboards, when they were at Brown Field in the early 1960s. That's Dennis Choate in the background—he became a famous Trans-Pacific boat builder. We were horsing around on the north side of the pier." (Courtesy of Mike Richardson.)

# Three

# THE BEACH TOWNS

The beach towns include breaks that were probably the first regularly surfed regions in San Diego. Ocean Beach, Old Mission Beach, and Pacific Beach lured heavy crowds during the summers and were home to many enthusiastic beachgoers. The reliable reef breaks of Sunset Cliffs and Tourmaline Street were quickly recognized as coveted surfing areas. In this photograph, the six Sunset Cliffs regulars posing with their boards are, from left to right, Kimball Daun, Rob Nelson, Bill Sayles, Joe Tody, Lloyd Baker, and Bill "Hadji" Hein. Lloyd, a gifted athlete, made some of the most sought-after surfboards in San Diego. He and Kimball could see the surf from their music appreciation class at Point Loma High School, and, one by one, the boys would disappear on a good surf day. The teachers were not pleased, but that is how much the youths were into surfing. If they weren't doing it, they were thinking about doing it. (Courtesy of Kimball Daun.)

A group of young friends hangs out in front of a 10¢ hamburger stand near the Old Mission Beach bathhouse. The bunch of 1934 beach buddies pictured here are, from left to right, (first row) Bill Klein, Delores Bunt, John "Peadunk" Kincy, Earl "Gogi" Russell, and Wharfy Hewitt; (second row) Roy Penwarden, Dixie Card, two unidentified girls, and lifeguard Bill Rumsey, wearing a hat and whistle. (Courtesy of Emil Sigler.)

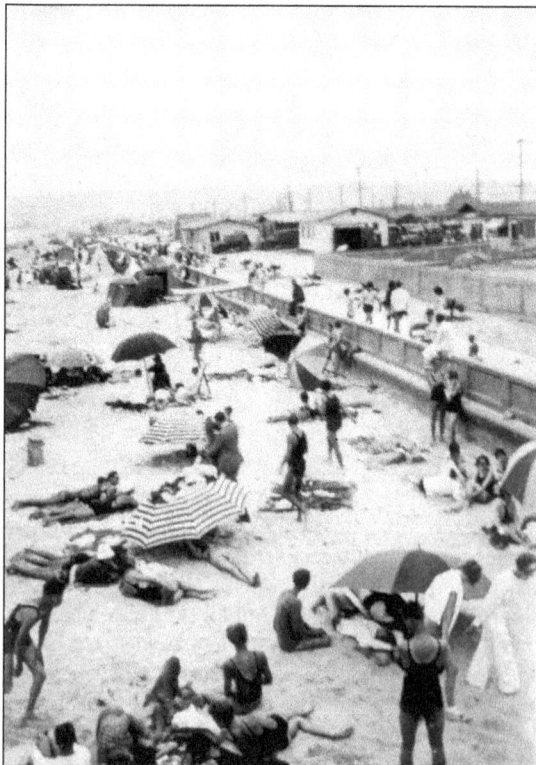

Taken from the lifeguard tower at Old Mission Beach on July 4, 1928, this photograph shows what a popular summer holiday destination this stretch of sandy beach has been for decades. The original boardwalk is pictured in the background. (Courtesy of Emil Sigler.)

Born and raised in Galveston, Texas, young Dorian Paskowitz moved with his family to San Diego in 1934. Known to the locals simply as "Tex," he was a strong presence in San Diego's surfing scene and became a city lifeguard from 1937 to 1941. Tex's first surfboard in San Diego was Charlie Wright's old board. Tex later crafted a Tom Blake–style hollow paddleboard with help from mentor Emil Sigler. In 1938, Tex paid $85 for a "more modern" custom, 50-pound solid balsa surfboard shaped by legendary Santa Monica–based waterman Preston "Pete" Peterson. A dynamic free spirit in his day, Tex wholly embraced surfing's alternative lifestyle and stressed health, fitness, and nutrition. Says Tex (later known as "Doc" after earning a medical degree from Stanford in 1946): "I learned to accept myself for what I was a long time ago—not good or bad, not a hero or a coward, just a surfer. I figured that was good enough." (Courtesy of SDHS.)

Members of the San Diego Surfing Club meet in 1940 to discuss the possibility of building a storage facility for their surf gear in Pacific Beach. Members pictured here are, from left to right, (first row) unidentified, Hadji Hein, Bill Nelson (with Noodles the dog), Emil Sigler, and Don Pritchard; (second row) Jack Prodanovich, Dick "Storm Surf" Taylor, Tex Paskowitz, Lloyd Baker, and Bill Sayles; (third row) Dempsey Holder, Jack Palmer, Raymond "Skeeter" Malcolm, Kimball Daun, and Roy Penwarden. (Courtesy of Bill Hein.)

Pulled from a 1938 spread in the *San Diego Union*, the caption reads: "A group of local paddleboard enthusiasts has introduced a new sport, paddleboard water polo, to the winter program at Mission Beach Plunge. Body blocking and other rough tactics play an important part in the game, patterned after regulation polo. Taking part in the demonstration . . . are, from left to right, Jack Prodanovich, Lloyd Baker (falling), and Lee Grady. Kimball Daun is blocked from view. The sport has been introduced to stimulate interest in the new plunge venture." (Courtesy of Bill Hein.)

Freddie Crowther took this stunning photograph of Tex Paskowitz catching air as he leaps for a ball being passed by "Young" Grady during an intense game of paddleboard water polo at the Mission Beach Plunge. According to Hadji Hein, "The boards took a beating, and so did we—it was a rough game. Our trunks were made from that scratchy tight-knit wool. We called them 'Smitties'." (Courtesy of Bill Hein.)

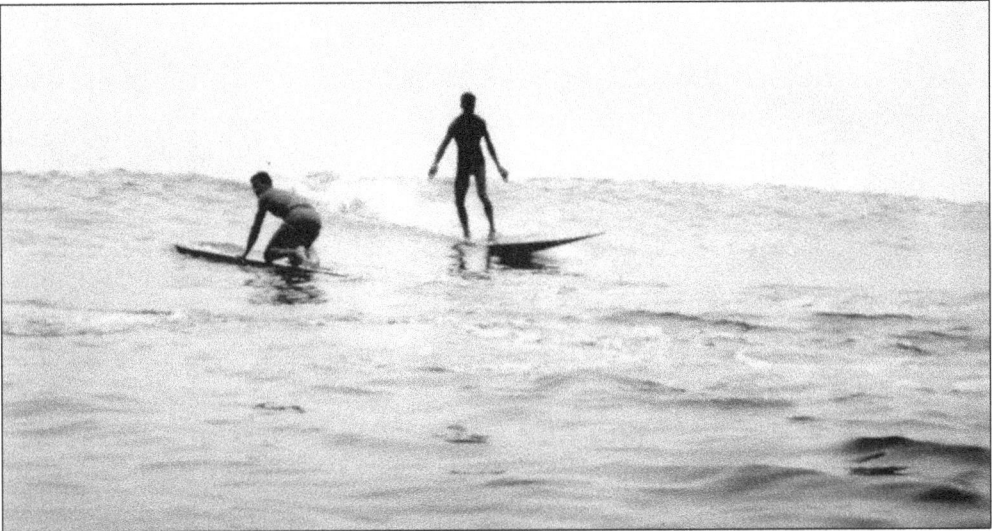

Two unidentified riders trade waves near Tourmaline Street in the 1930s. According to author Robert Baxley: "The early surfers became accomplished rough water swimmers because they spent a lot of time swimming after their boards. Many became excellent lifeguards due to the strength and first-hand knowledge of waves and currents gained through their surfing adventures." (Courtesy of Emil Sigler.)

Don Okey provided the materials needed to construct this simple shack at Pacific Beach Point in 1938. During World War II, the point was known as "Gunnery Point" because the military had placed artillery on the site in case of enemy invasion. Before the shack was built, surfboards and gear were stored in nearby bushes, sometimes for weeks, until the surf came up. The small reef and cobblestone point break below offers a fantastic right-hand slide on solid winter swells, with rides sometimes stretching hundreds of yards to Tourmaline Street. (Courtesy of Maggie Okey.)

Four friends share a wave along the inside section of Pacific Beach Point. Pictured with the Point Loma peninsula in the background, these shadowy riders are, from left to right, Emil Sigler, Hadji Hein, Tex Paskowitz, and Lloyd Baker, regulars at the point and just about anywhere waves were being ridden in the region. (Courtesy of Emil Sigler.)

In 1940, the newly formed San Diego Surfing Club (SDSC) was active in promoting paddleboard water polo and organizing competitions between its members and clubs in Palos Verdes, Santa Monica, and elsewhere. A women's auxiliary, the Wahinis, began about the same time and helped the SDSC organize social and fund-raising events. In this photograph, Tex Paskowitz speaks to a large crowd in Pacific Beach to ask the city to allow the SDSC to build a permanent clubhouse to host their own meetings and functions. (Courtesy of Bill Hein.)

Bruce Westphal, a stylish surfer both on the waves and on the beach, rides Sunset Cliffs in the early 1950s. On this day, a couple of the guys paddled out with a Kodak camera wrapped in a plastic bag and took turns shooting pictures of each other. (Courtesy of Jim Robb.)

Raymond "Skeeter" Malcolm (left) stands with his dad, Marshall "Red" Malcolm, and brother Marsh "Scooter" Malcolm in front of the boys' boards at Sunset Cliffs in 1941. As a teacher and coach, Skeeter was one of San Diego's most influential surfing personalities, and hundreds of young men and women in the beach towns looked up to him. His passion for surfing lives on through his daughter Marilyn and son Steve. (Courtesy of Marsh Malcolm.)

Big brother Skeeter (left), who was already a powerful surfer, takes a much younger Marsh out on a cut-down board for his very first "real surf lesson." Their mother, Lola Mae ("Snooks"), took this photograph from the bluff at Sunset Cliffs. (Courtesy of Marsh Malcolm.)

Neighborhood kids hang out in the Malcolms' backyard in the early 1940s. Howard Danner (left), Joanne Hilbun, and Marsh Malcolm pose with the cart used to haul surfboards. Said Marsh, "My older brother, Skeeter, made this contraption for me so I would not have to drag my cut-down board to the beach. It had buggy wheels and a long wooden handle. I was kind of small, and we lived three-and-a-half blocks from the beach, so it came in real handy." (Courtesy of Marsh Malcolm.)

Ocean Beach lifeguard Gordon Penwarden relaxes with Burt Williams (left) and Jim "Mouse" Robb in 1946. Gordon helped supervise the youngsters while on the beach and taught them to swim and bodysurf. (Courtesy of Jim Robb.)

Mouse Robb stands proudly with the smaller-size surfboard he purchased from his good friend Marsh Malcolm for $5. Besides being Ocean Beach's best-known surfer and paddler, Mouse had a long and successful career as a lifeguard. He probably logged more rescues and saved more lives over the past 40 years than anyone around. (Courtesy of Jim Robb.)

Showing off their prized boards, surfers (from left to right) Jon Kowel, Mouse Robb, Bud Lewis, and Sonny Maggiore take a classic pose. "Storm Surf" Taylor made John's board, Mouse stands in front of the board he purchased from Marsh Malcolm for $5, Bud's board is from unknown origins, and Sonny has an old kook box once owned by Hoppy Swarts. (Courtesy of Jim Robb.)

From left to right, preteens Marsh Malcolm, Mouse Robb, and Bob Fieger shoulder their behemoth 45- to 55-pound surfboards to a surf session in 1948. These boards all had small skegs, or fins, fixed near the tail. When a nailed-on skeg was knocked off or loosened, the boys would grab a beach rock and pound the fin back on. (Courtesy of Jim Robb.)

Coronado surfers Tom Carlin and John Elwell lean against John's Ford "surfmobile" before a session at Sunset Cliffs in the early 1950s. Besides being an excellent surfer, Carlin later became an expert diver and navy frogman. (Courtesy of John Elwell.)

Sunset Cliffs provided some of the best, most consistent surf in all San Diego. Getting down to the breaks, however, was another matter. One could start out in the water from Ocean Beach and make the long paddle south, or one could come down the cliffs by the Theosophical Society. These local surfers standing at the base of the obtrusive cliffs in 1950 are, from left to right, Marsh Malcolm, Mike Considine, Lance Morton, Mouse Robb, Bud Lewis, and Don Mellon. (Courtesy of Bud Caldwell.)

The winners of the 1954 San Diego City Lifeguard Relays give triumphant smiles. This event was so closely contested that less than one minute separated first and last place. Here John Largent mans the oars in the stern of the dory, accompanied by Fred Thompson and Roger Grady. (Courtesy of Evelyn Largent.)

John Largent demonstrates an old version of wake surfing on his prized Gordon & Smith (G&S) surfboard at Bass Lake in 1963. His wife, Evelyn, took the picture as she sat in *Honey Boy*, their 17-foot inboard-driven motorboat that John built in his garage some years earlier. (Courtesy of Evelyn Largent.)

La Jolla High School coed Dolly Clint poses in her new Catalina two-piece bathing suit at Mission Beach in 1948. Dolly grew up around surfers but never seriously considered it for herself. She recalls, "Most of the girls who went to the beach in those days didn't surf—the boards were just too big, too wide, too heavy. We were more than content to watch the boys." Dolly later married local craftsman and waterman Robert "Black Mac" McClendon. (Courtesy of Mac McClendon.)

Six lovelies strike an artistic pose in this late-1940s photograph while performing synchronized routines on paddleboards. Special aqua events were held at various locations in Mission Beach and La Jolla, no doubt partly inspired by popular Esther Williams movies of the time. (Courtesy of Terry Curren.)

Pictured here in 1953 near Old Mission Beach, Mary Jean Cooley McCandless, all of 5 feet 2 inches and 102 pounds soaking wet, poses with her 11-foot balsa shaped by Bob Simmons. She had originally seen surfing in Hawaii and promptly took up the sport after arriving in San Diego a year earlier. Mary Jean broke her nose on a big wave in Del Mar when her loose board smashed her square in the face. Undaunted, she pushed the cartilage back in place and went back out to catch more waves. Her love of the ocean continued down through her family. (Courtesy of Cathleen McCandless.)

Norma Jean Malcolm (left) and Ed "Blackie" Hoffman share a wave in Ocean Beach in the late 1960s. Norma Jean Malcolm was a champion water-skier before her husband, Marsh, urged her to learn to surf. At the time, Blackie was a sander at Burland Surf Shop, one of the area's first surf retailers. (Courtesy of Marsh Malcolm.)

Surfers have always been creative when devising methods to get their heavy, unwieldy boards down to the beach. This unidentified Pacific Beach local built a rack for his bicycle using old wagon wheels.

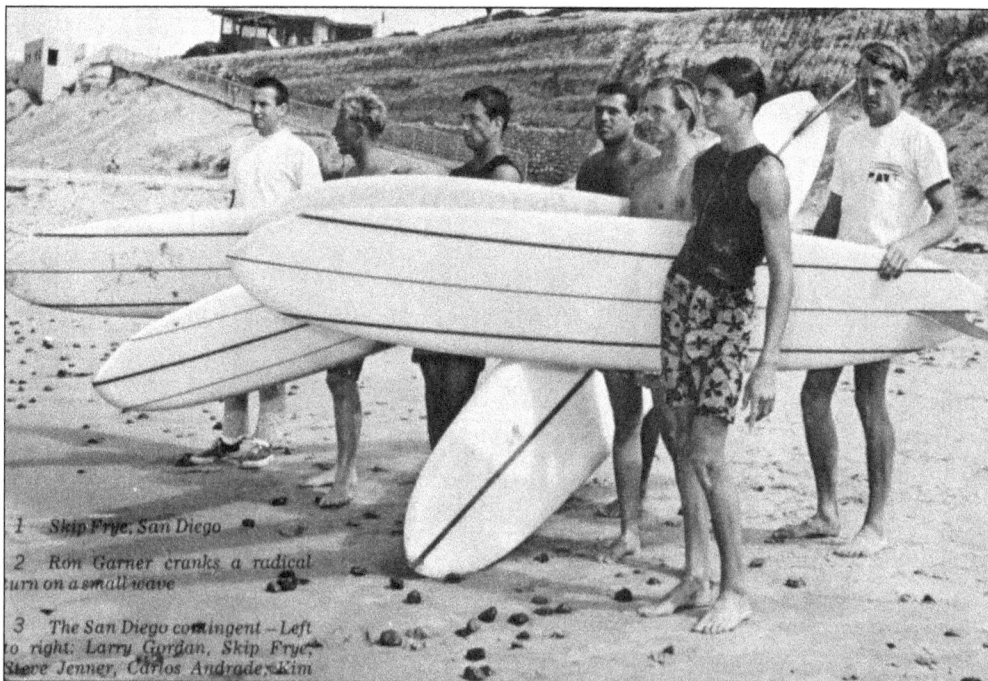

Larry Gordon (left) and Floyd Smith, longtime friends from Pacific Beach Junior High, started surfing together in 1955. Together they formed the highly regarded Gordon & Smith Surfboards (G&S) label. The San Diego contingent of the G&S surf team featured in this photograph are, from left to right, Larry Gordon, Skip Frye, Steve Jenner, Carlos Andrade, unidentified, Larry Estrada, and Skip Wright.

46

# Surfing Club

Organized to recognize and promote surfing as a sport was the main purpose of this club.

Under the sponsorship of Mr. Malcolm the Surfing Club has undertaken such actitivities as weekend trips, an inter-club surfing contest, campus sales and a school movie.

MR. MALCOLM
Advisor

AL PORTER
President

A 1964 photograph of Crawford High School's Surfing Club boasts 43 members, Marsh Malcolm as its advisor, weekend trips, and a school movie. Crawford was one of San Diego's first inland schools to promote surfing. (Courtesy of Marsh Malcolm.)

Marsh Malcolm is locked in the curl at Ocean Beach during the late 1950s. Marsh is wearing an early wet suit—a cumbersome, modified diving suit called a "beavertail" that helped keep surfers warmer when the water temperature dropped below 60 degrees. (Courtesy of Marsh Malcolm.)

Mouse Robb hoists Judy Dibble overhead during practices for an upcoming tandem surfing contest in 1959. The pair competed frequently in several big events, from Malibu to Ocean Beach, and competed against the best tandem teams of the era. As Mouse recalls, "Well, it certainly was one way to pick up girls!" (Courtesy of Jim Robb.)

Winners display their trophies after a 1963 surf contest at Crystal Pier in Pacific Beach. Contestants included, from left to right, (first row) Billy Brummett, Hank Warner, and Judy Dibble; (second row) Dale Dobson, Jon Close, Skip Frye, and Butch Van Artsdalen. Dale Dobson has been one of the most enduring competitors in the realm of surfing, winning titles in all major categories, including knee boarding. (Courtesy of Diana Brummett.)

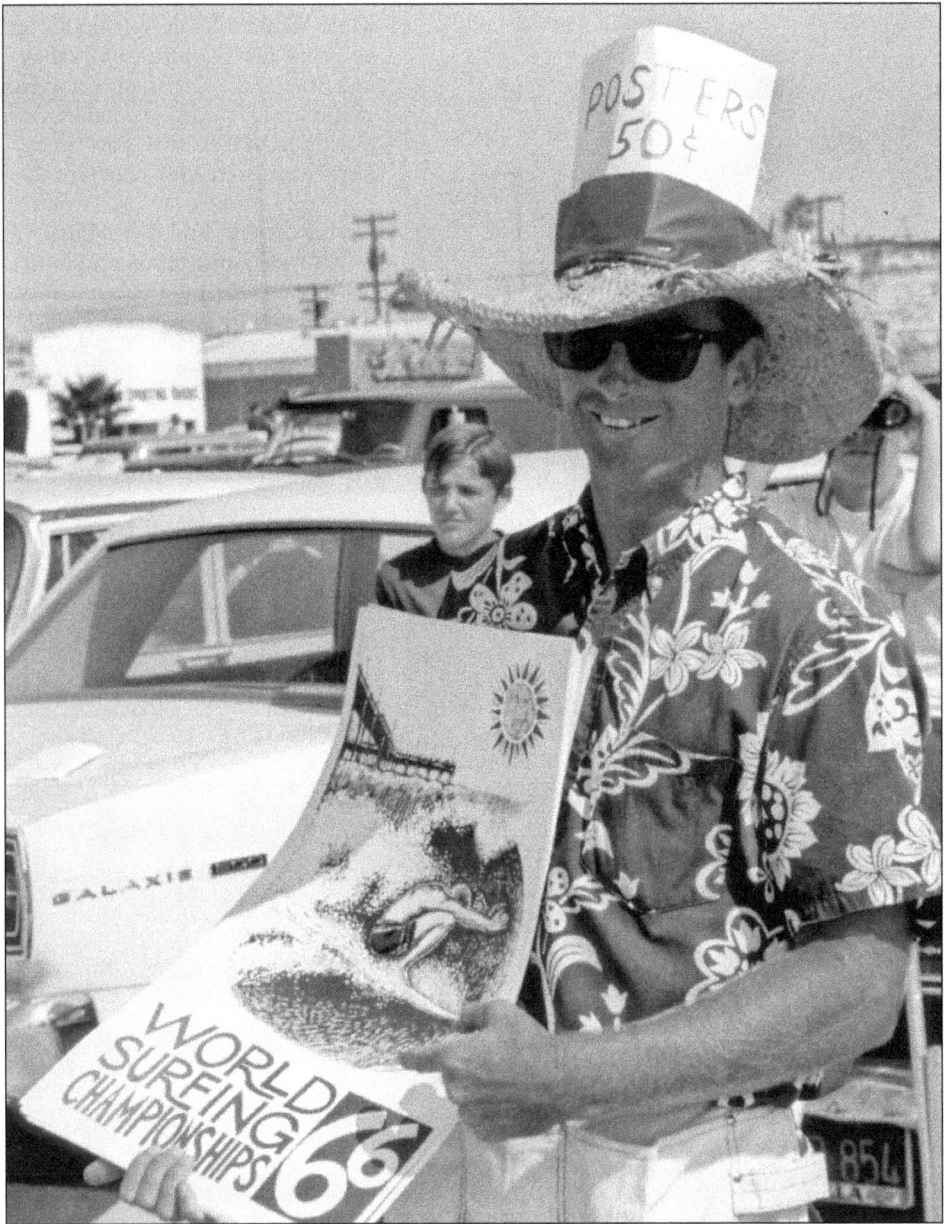

Tommy Carlin sells posters for the 1966 World Contest for just 50¢ each. The world championship contest was highly organized and enthusiastically backed by the city of San Diego as well as the entire surfing community. World Contest chairman Hevs McClelland stated, "This is shaping up as the greatest surfing contest ever held. It's going to be incredible how many fantastically talented international surfers will be clustered along one stretch of coastline for the weeklong competition. We want to make sure that every competitor has plenty of time in the water, and we will have tested him under the most challenging and varied conditions possible. Essentially, the top men and women stars will be tested in three separate contests: reef break, point break, and beach break. Competition is set up on a mobile basis—wherever the coast offers the best conditions for that day is where the action is. The finals will be held at Ocean Beach, in front of cameras manned by ABC's Wide World of Sports." (Photograph by Tom Keck.)

Kimo Wilder McVay (left) looks on as Billy Riley-Watkins gets a quick kiss from Duke Kahanamoku in front of the world contest headquarters on Shelter Island. At first, San Diego city leaders were very reluctant to host such a risky event as a world surfing contest, and it was Miss Billy's vision, insistence, and hard work that made the event a reality. (Courtesy of Billy Riley-Watkins.)

Skip Frye trims through one of his heats at the 1966 World Contest in Ocean Beach. Skip, one of San Diego's most celebrated surfers and shapers, took up the sport of kings during his junior year at Mission Bay High School. Low-key and modest, Skip allows his custom surfboards and controlled surfing style to speak about his abilities. (Photograph by Tom Keck.)

David Nuuhiwa was considered to be one of the world's top nose riders, and here he exhibits the classic pose that made him instantly recognizable. In the head-to-head rivalry with Nat Young, one of the huge moments of the competition was David's breathtaking, 10-second nose ride, captured forever on film by ace cameraman Ron Stoner.

Linda Benson walks to the nose at Ocean Beach during the 1966 World Contest. Her quickness and athletic ability allowed her to excel in the tricky hotdog maneuvers, like riding the nose, that were popular at the time. (Photograph by Ron Church.)

Young Australian surfing phenom Nat Young rides his special board, "Magic Sam," during a heat at the 1966 World Contest in Ocean Beach. "Magic Sam" was a thin, 9-foot 4-inch squaretail with a George Greenough–inspired fin—a radical design for the time. At the competition's end, Nat captured the men's world title and trophy for his Down Under homeland. (Photograph by Tom Keck.)

Nineteen-year-old Joyce Hoffman exhibits style and poise on her way to a first-place finish at the World Contest in Ocean Beach. With the victory, Joyce became surfing's first two-time, back-to-back world champion. She was pictured on the cover of *Life* magazine and featured in *Seventeen*, *Look*, *Sports Illustrated*, *Teen*, and *Vogue*. The *Los Angeles Times* also named Joyce the sporting world's "Woman of the Year." (Photograph by Tom Keck.)

# *Four*

# LA JOLLA

Those who surfed north of Tourmaline in the 1920s and 1930s favored La Jolla Shores, La Jolla Cove, and even Big Rock. It was not until 1937, though, when Woodridge "Woody" Parker Brown III rode a wave at Windansea, that most others realized the possibilities of the local reefs. About 15 years later, it was by coincidence that another Woody—Jack "Woody" Ekstrom—snapped this memorable picture of Deane Carlson struggling to wrest his plank from the jaws of the Windansea shore break in 1952. On this day, the peak was outside and the tide was coming in just as Woody happened by with "Doc" John Ball's "waterbox" camera. One snap was all it took. (Courtesy of Woody Ekstrom.)

Clyde F. Bobzin sits on the steps leading to the Windansea Hotel at Playa del Sur in La Jolla. The original hotel structure was taken over and renamed the Windansea Hotel by the Snell family in the early 1920s. It became a very popular resort and dining destination until it was lost to a fire in 1943. (Courtesy of the Bobzin family.)

Don (left) and Pat Bobzin had small-scale paddleboards that they used in the waters off La Jolla. Both the locals and the tourists enjoyed annual rough water swims, aquaplaning, and paddleboard races from the Scripps Pier to the Main Cove. (Courtesy of the Bobzin family.)

Jack Lounsberry, age 11, catches soup at La Jolla Shores in 1938. He was inspired to try surfing after watching Don Okey and Woody Brown. Jack ordered a 10-foot balsa and redwood surfboard from McCall Sporting Goods for $17, which was eventually made and shipped down from Pacific Systems Homes in Long Beach. Jack, who also helped build the first shack at Windansea, has been surfing that hallowed break since 1940. (Courtesy of Jack Lounsberry.)

Aquaplaning, freeboarding, water-skiing, and speedboat rides were ways that locals could do some thrill seeking in San Diego's waters as well as show the tourists some adventure. Phil Barber had a glass-bottom boat and used to drive folks to Devil's Slide to show them the rich variety of marine life at the cove. Charles Fleming advertised his boating services at the nearby beach club and had a thriving business. (Courtesy of Woody Ekstrom.)

Woody Ekstrom is enjoying a north swell at the cove in the fall of 1944. Woody purchased this Lloyd Baker–shaped board from John Fowler for $7.50 and hauled it from Pacific Beach to La Jolla by cart. (Courtesy of Woody Ekstrom.)

In 1948, La Jolla lifeguard Ken Haygood takes his redwood and balsa board out for an early-morning paddle before the crowd arrives. Then, as now, lifeguards paddled out or took a swim to stay in condition. Abalone, lobster, and fish were plentiful, and lifeguards waited until after their shifts to dive for dinner. (Courtesy of Ken Haygood.)

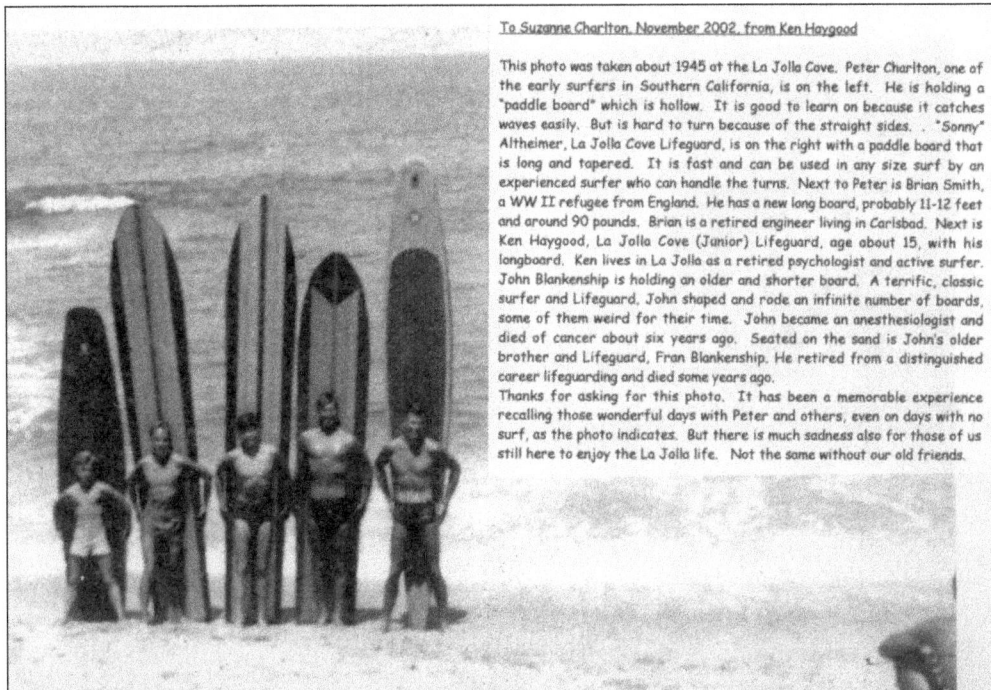

Dr. Kenneth Haygood, seen in the middle of this 1945 lineup at the cove, provided the recollection at the far right. (Courtesy of Kenneth Haygood.)

Young Brian Smith (left), an English refugee from the bombings of London during World War II, and Ken Haygood display the day's catch of 5 lobsters and 12 abalones (abs). The abs are laid out on an old nylon target retrieved by local surfers after it had been shot down during gunnery practice off Pacific Beach Point. The lobsters were donated to a sunset luau on the beach, and Ken sold the abs to a local restaurant for 35¢ apiece. He would have taken them home, but the last time he did his mom said, "Oh no, not abalone again! Can't you just bring home some nice fresh fish?" (Courtesy of Ken Haygood.)

"AFTER SURFING"
Brian Smith & Ken Haygood
1945, Cove

One fine day in 1945, Ken Haygood ditched his physical education class at La Jolla High School for this session at Windansea. Ken went on to graduate with the class of 1946 and eventually secured his Ph.D. from the University of Chicago. (Courtesy of Ken Haygood.)

Buzzy Bent (left) rides a balsa board shaped by Joe Quigg, as Dempsey Holder (center) and Bobby Ekstrom share the same wave in 1949. From the day Buzzy showed up at Windansea, he amazed the locals by doing bottom turns, redirecting his surfboard at the bottom of a wave, which no one had ever seen. (Courtesy of Woody Ekstrom.)

One can go left . . . since Windansea breaks both right and left over a flat rock, but locals know taking the rip back out after the ride in saves a little energy. It wasn't until 1937, when Woody Brown took off at Windansea, that others realized it was possible to conquer the break. Not a surfing spot for the faint of heart, differing conditions in tide and weather make for challenging situations. The regulars wouldn't have it any other way. (Photograph by Joe Quigg.)

Or one can go right . . . since north swells can produce decent rights and nice, long rides. Originally called Neptune Beach, Windansea got its name from the old hotel across the way that was owned by the Snell family. In 1946, Don Okey and a handful of volunteers constructed a timber and palm frond shack that provided shade from the afternoon sun and was strong enough to support their heavy wooden planks. The San Diego Historical Site Board added the shack to its official register in 1998. (Courtesy of Woody Ekstrom.)

1948 Woody Brown

| | |
|---|---|
| Length | 11'1" |
| Nose | 13.75" |
| Tail | 11" |
| Width | 23.25" |
| Thickness | 2.80" |
| Fin | 2.75" Keel |

Balsa/Redwood. Varnish-sealed.
Owned and surfed by Townsend "Towny"
Cromwell, Towny brought this board to La
Jolla in 1951. Features a concave deck,
rolled rails and an extremely pulled tail.

New York native Woody Brown stands with an early hot curl shape he was experimenting with in the late 1940s. This balsa and redwood board represented a leap forward in big-wave surfboard design at the time, as Woody and several Hawaiian shapers were challenged to meet the requirements necessary to tackle the formidable waves of Oahu's North Shore. As a youth who hung out at Long Island's Curtis Airfield in the 1920s and counted Charles Lindbergh among his friends, Woody understood a great deal about flight. His passion led him to become a world champion glider pilot. By 1935, when he relocated to La Jolla, Woody was able to apply many aerodynamic techniques and theories of lift to surfboard design. While his buddies were building solid wooden planks, Woody was creating a hollow board, 4 inches thick and at just more than 9 feet in length. Around 1936, he constructed another hollow board, this time a little thinner, longer, and wider, at about nine pounds and with a V-bottom. He also added something almost unheard of at the time in surfing—a skeg, or fin—allowing him to lean into his turns the way it is done today. (Photograph by Woody Ekstrom.)

Townsend "Towny" Cromwell was one of the first surfers in La Jolla. He and Woody Brown were passionate about surfing and had an enduring love of and endless curiosity about all things ocean-related. Towny worked for the U.S. Fish and Wildlife Service, often going on long cruises aboard various research vessels. The Cromwell Current, a fish migration path he discovered emanating off the coast of South America, is named for him.

Walter Roach took this photograph of five good friends getting ready for a day's surf at Windansea in 1946. These pioneers that the younger set looked up to and admired are, from left to right, Towny Cromwell, Buddy Hull, Woody Ekstrom, Bill Isenhouer, and Andy Forshaw. (Courtesy of Woody Ekstrom.)

Fashioned after much-admired Hawaiian beach culture, the annual luaus at Windansea were held between 1946 and the early 1950s. Don Okey worked long hours to coordinate the entire event, procure the food, and supervise the cooking. The barbeques might be above ground or in deep pits in the sand. In this photograph, fresh timber, palm fronds, and flowers have just been delivered in preparation for the 1947 event. (Courtesy of Terry Curren.)

Well-known commercial artist Jack Boillard painted the poster of Hoppy Swarts, announcing the upcoming luau festivities, seen in this 1947 photograph. At left, volunteer workers prepare the meat to roast in the pit area. The word was out, and the luau was officially on the way. (Courtesy of Woody Ekstrom.)

The hugely popular Hawaiian-style luaus were only held for a few years, but surfers appeared from up and down the coast to partake in the free feast, music, and liquid refreshments. The size of the crowds began to cause some concern for the local officials, and, too soon, they became a thing of the past. (Courtesy of Woody Ekstrom.)

Each luau took on a distinctly island flavor. Palm fronds and flowers covered the shack, pigs or sheep were roasted on the beach, Hawaiian attire was encouraged, and music reigned supreme. Everett "E. J." Oshier, from San Clemente, is on guitar, and his wife, Jo, is seated next to him. Sitting next to Jo is Hollywood actor James Arness, who was a surfing regular at San Onofre and whose son Rolf became the world's surfing champion in 1970. (Courtesy of E. J. Oshier.)

From left to right, friends Don Okey, John Blankenship, and Buddy Hull were highly respected surfers and innovators at Windansea. In this 1945 photograph, they all share a wave, respecting each other's place and not competing for space, simply moving in sync across the wave. (Photograph by Bob McGowan.)

Buddy Hull (right) looks back to keep an eye on Don Okey's soon-to-be-loose 85-pound surfboard. As Ken Haygood recalls, " 'Pearling,' when you went nose-first, straight down, meant that the board would go straight up. You had to dive under water and go as deep as possible to give the board time to come down. The next wave often took the board ashore, sometimes against rocks and reefs. You, then, had to bodysurf in and hope somebody had pulled your board up on the sand." (Photograph by Bob McGowan.)

Born in La Mesa and raised in La Jolla, Don Okey designed and built the first shacks at Pacific Beach Point and Windansea, and organized and ran the splendid annual luaus. A strong surfer and paddler, he was in the top 10 finishers at the Pacific Coast Championships from 1939 to 1941. He and John Blankenship experimented with foam boards in the early 1950s, perfecting the chemistry and process until they had some rideable boards. In the 1960s, Don invented a shaping machine that turned out hundreds of local boards. To this day, the shack at Windansea, designated in 1998 as an official historic site, stands as testament to Don Okey's passion for the ocean and surfing. In this photograph, Don is victorious in the 1948 Oceanside Pier Paddleboard Race. He had been cruising the coast looking for good surf when he heard about the event. When he crossed the finish line, he was so far ahead of the pack that most of the nearest competitors had not even rounded the pier. (Courtesy of Maggie Okey.)

This version of the shack, seen here in 1953, was rebuilt after storm damage but lacks the changing room and board locker that the 1945 model had. The small board leaning upright belonged to Windansea regular Tommy Hederman, an accomplished waterman and surfer who happened to be a dwarf. (Courtesy of Woody Ekstrom.)

Looking south from the sandy beach at Windansea, several beachgoers seem to be staring at the local surfers and their boards. The small sandwich-board sign seen at far right reads: "Danger . . . Surfing Area . . . Beware of Loose Boards." (Courtesy of Woody Ekstrom.)

John Elwell stands beside his Simmons board in 1952. The boards pictured are balsa and fiberglass, the forerunners of modern hydrodynamic design. Varnished wood surfboards disappeared along with hollow paddleboards because they became obsolete. Foam surfboards began to arrive with the post–World War II improved technology. The surfers at Windansea were often at the forefront of design and innovation. (Courtesy of John Elwell.)

Carl Knox (left) and Peter Parkin lounge against Carl's 1929 Plymouth on Nautilus Street in the early 1950s. Peter was a very skilled surfer, and it was in his garage, nicknamed "Parkin's Palace," that locals first built a different kind of board—one that sported wheels. Still, it took several years before sidewalk surfing became a sensation. (Courtesy of Carl Knox.)

Bob Simmons is captured streaking across a solid wall in Malibu during the summer of 1949. Note his board's long wake, indicative of the pure speed his signature surfboards were known for. Photographs of Bob surfing are very rare, but he gave this snapshot of himself to John Elwell many years ago. The photographer remains unidentified. (Courtesy of John Elwell.)

Bob Simmons talks surf and board theory at the foot of Marine Street on January 9, 1954. The surf was unrideable and breaking 20 feet at the La Jolla Cove. Bob usually dressed comfortably; younger surfers readily adapted to the plaid flannel shirts and casual pants he favored. Pictured here from left to right are Bob, Tom Carlin, Jim Nesbitt, and Johnny Linden. (Courtesy of John Elwell.)

A 1950 Simmons board rests in the tidal sand, representing its lost rider. Simmons made only about 200 of these remarkable boards, each with his signature hydrodynamic features, less weight, and resined fiberglass exteriors. The boards are highly valued today. Simmons met his fate at Windansea on September 26, 1954. It was a day of big surf, and several observers on the beach, including Mike Diffenderfer, Carl Ekstrom, and Ronald Patterson, noticed that Simmons had been knocked off his board by a formidable set. Surging whitewater minimized visibility, and no one paid much attention until a local youngster retrieved Simmons's board and pulled it up on the beach. The surfing community went numb with shock. His body washed ashore a few days later. (Photograph by John Elwell.)

Windansea regulars pose with their boards at the shack in 1951. Two very early John Blankenship foam boards are seen at far right and third from right. Surfers are, from left to right, (first row) Don Anderson, Dick Wynn, Carl Knox, and Steve Gray; (second row) Jerry Robinson, Don Russell, Allan Cunningham, Ralph Cox, Mike Tellep, Buzzy Bent, Bob Gutowski, and Billy Males. (Courtesy of Carl Knox.)

Carl Knox rides his board, shaped by Dale Velzy, at Windansea in 1960. Nine years earlier, Carl and Billy Males had taken the first successful foam boards that John Blankenship built to Hawaii, where the new technology and materials caused quite a stir. (Courtesy of Carl Knox.)

Two of the top Windansea surfers of their era, Pat Curren (right) and Ronald Patterson share a pensive moment at the beach. Pat's keen sense of observation served him well when he moved to Hawaii to surf the world's biggest waves and shape the boards best suited to tame them. (Courtesy of Terry Curren.)

Tom,
Best Wishes
Aloha, Killer
Dana Surf Shop

Windansea surfers pose for a casual photograph in 1957. Pictured are, from left to right, (first row) Tweak Cheney, Danny Prall, and unidentified; (second row) Butch Van Artsdalen, Pat Curren, Ronald Patterson, Chuck Hasley, and Del Cannon. (Courtesy of Terry Curren.)

San Diego artists Mike Dormer and Lee Teacher created a nose-heavy, beer-bellied, mop-headed icon in an early-1960s cartoon strip for *Scavenger* magazine, and surfing's pop philosopher was born. Then, in 1963, Lee carried things one step further by constructing a larger-than-life statue from found materials and concrete. He and Mike hauled the finished icon down to Windansea late one night, carved out a base in a rock, and cemented "Hot Curl" in place. After much controversy and consternation, city officials deemed the statue structurally sound, and a party was scheduled to celebrate it. Nationwide media interest was high, and large numbers of onlookers attended the official dedication. However, just two weeks after Hot Curl's installation ceremony, the impish icon was attacked, mutilated, and decapitated. Legend has it that the vandalism was committed by one of Windansea's most pugilistic locals. Lee Louis took this 16-mm footage of Hot Curl at the statue's official debut for part of a KFSD-TV (now KGTV/10 News) on-the-spot story. (Courtesy of Lee Louis.)

Hot Curl stands sentinel over Windansea as Anna Ekstrom Deneen, on vacation from Minnesota to visit her family, watches over her son Daniel. A few days following this picture, a disgruntled Windansea regular reduced the Hot Curl statue to a headless pile of rubble. (Courtesy of Woody Ekstrom.)

The Hot Curl cartoons appeared in all three issues of the short-lived *Scavenger* magazine, around 1958 and 1959. Plastic models of the scrawny character were available by mail order from the surfing publications. Creator Mike Dormer described his likeable leading man as "pure of heart, with a sort of flawed innocence," definitely an embodiment of late-1950s anti-establishment sympathies that surfers were partial to. (Courtesy of Mike Dormer.)

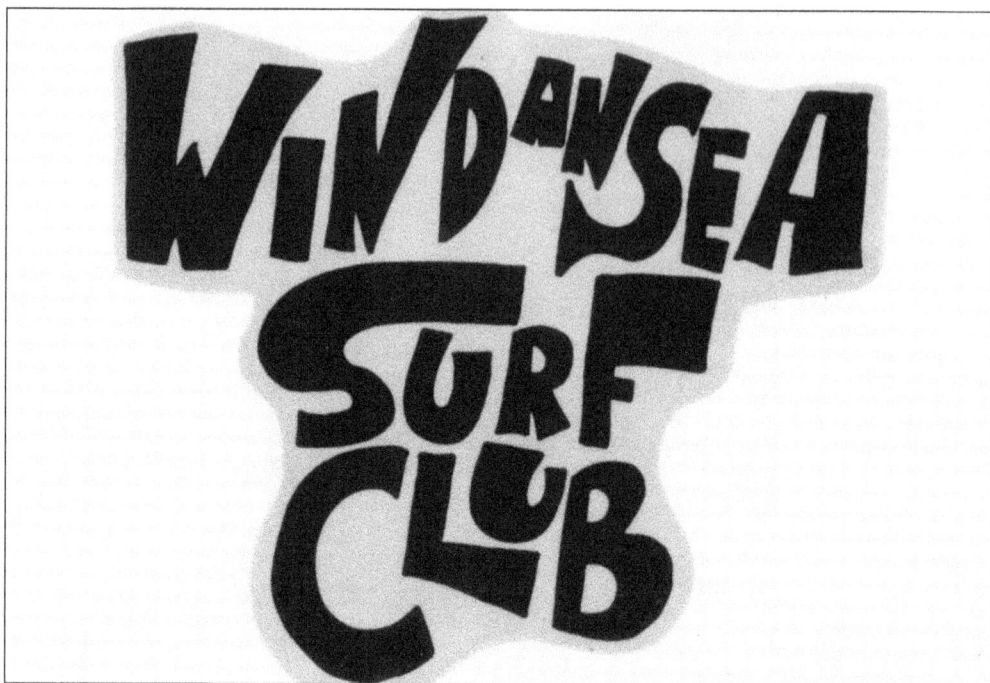

Bruce Cornelius created the current logo of the revitalized Windansea Surf Club on the bus trip the team took to the Malibu Invitational in 1963. Bruce reportedly did the lettering with a red felt-tip pen directly onto the T-shirt. (Courtesy of Lee Louis.)

The talent-laden Windansea Surf Club gathers during an outing at Moonlight Beach in 1963. Soon after this photograph was taken, some of the boys flew off to an invitational contest at Makaha. Some of the most widely known surf legends in the world appear in this photograph, from Hobie Alter and Linda Benson to Mike Diffenderfer and Skip Frye. (Photograph by Lee Louis.)

Victors at the classic confrontation at Malibu in 1963, the Windansea competitors are pictured with their trophies. The club had hired a bus to take them north for the weekend and placed five surfers in the six-man final. (Courtesy of Mike Burner.)

In 1964, for the second year in a row, the Windansea team traveled to Oahu for the Makaha Invitational contest. Dale Dobson (first row, third from left) seems to be talking over his shoulder with Duke Kahanamoku, honorary chairman of the event. (Photograph by Tom Keck.)

Joey Cabell (left) visits with Mickey Munoz (center) and Chuck Hasley at Moonlight Beach in 1963. Mickey was one of the most innovative surfers around, inventing such moves as the "Mysterioso" and the "Quasimoto." Chuck had just revived the dormant Windansea Club in order to compete in the Malibu Invitational. (Photograph by Lee Louis.)

Mike Hynson is one of the top nose riders of all time. A masterful shaper and innovator, he created the popular Red Fin signature model for Gordon & Smith Surfboards. A stylish and confident trendsetter, Mike will forever be remembered as the costar (with Robert August) of Bruce Brown's classic movie The Endless Summer.

Bobby Patterson (left) shares an anecdote with younger brother Ronnie Patterson and Butch Van Artsdalen (center) at Tourmaline. The three Patterson brothers, who also included Raymond, came from Hawaii in the 1950s and epitomized the beach-boy lifestyle. (Photograph by Lee Louis.)

Butch Van Artsdalen is the charismatic personality that is most identified with Windansea. His family moved to La Jolla in 1955, and Butch soon discovered surfing. An incredibly gifted athlete, he lettered in football, baseball, and track for three years at La Jolla High School. From the day he followed Carl Ekstrom into the surf at Windansea, Butch was such a natural that the trickiest maneuvers, such as the switch-stance position, seemed almost effortless to him, leaving many regulars feeling frustrated.

Ricky Grigg swings it left on a good day at Black's in 1965. At home in the ocean for most of his life, Ricky was studying marine biology at Scripps Institute and spending as much time surfing Black's as he could. (Photograph by Ron Church.)

Dickie Moon commits to a full-rail bottom turn on a bumpy day at La Jolla Shores in 1967. The Shores is one of the only beaches in the county that is not affected by winds from the south, and Dickie was known as one of the top surfers there. (Photograph by Tom Keck.)

Photographer Ron Church captures Chuck O'Grady in a regal pose on a classic day at Windansea in 1964. Ron was one of the first San Diego photographers to go into the water, and his images portrayed surfing moments with an intimacy and artistry not seen before. (Photograph by Ron Church.)

Ron Church shared his vast knowledge of underwater photography and marine life with the world. For more than 20 years, Ron captured oceanic images for Scripps Institute as well as Jacques Cousteau's *Calypso* diving team. Several of Ron's distinct surf photographs are featured in his fantastic books, *CA/HI* and *Surf Contest*. (Courtesy of Tani Church Bell.)

La Jolla native Carl Ekstrom has always applied his mind to the sport he loves—surfing. A designer, inventor, and consummate craftsman, Carl's main legacy may be the asymmetrical surfboard. Developed in 1963, the asymmetrical shape reflected the combination of a regular board's plan shape with that of a semi-gun's. (Photograph by Lynn Fayman; courtesy of Carl Ekstrom.)

Youngsters look up to three of the most respected La Jolla surfers of their day. Standing from left to right are Dr. John Blankenship, Carl Ekstrom, and Don Russell. La Jolla entrepreneurs Carol Baker and Clara Jo Brown used this photograph in a calendar they put together in the late 1970s featuring significant area personalities. "We also wanted to show the younger generation that some of our finest surfers had matured along with the sport." (Photograph by Clara Jo Brown; courtesy of Carl Ekstrom.)

Al Nelson, pictured here at Windansea in the early 1960s, made his mark early on as an innovative, talented shaper. He built balsa surfboards for the locals, and others came from up and down the coast for his boards. Al used the shack as his base of operations, as did Pat Curren and David Cheney, until the day an errant match ignited the balsa shavings and almost burned it down. (Photograph by Tom Keck.)

Mike Diffenderfer, one of the most capable craftsmen in an area known for its talented shapers, cuts back on a La Jolla wave. Raised in La Jolla, his early shaping career was influenced by Pat Curren, and Mike was one of the first surfer/shapers to recognize the importance of a rocker—the board's nose-to-tail curve—in overall surfboard performance. He later relocated to Hawaii, where his big-wave guns became highly prized. (Photograph by Tom Keck.)

"In the early 1960s John Donnelly and I 'discovered' Black's one day when Scripps wasn't really breaking but we could see sets up the coast," recalls Greg Hogan. "When we got up to the road we stopped and were blown away by amazing, peeling waves with no one on them. After a two-hour session, we knew we had found THE SPOT. And, we had it all to ourselves. We board-and-bodysurfed great waves there year-round and it was rare to ever see anyone else out. In the winter it was always easy to build a beach fire to keep warm because there was so much driftwood around. Much later we fully appreciated the fact that Black's is a world class wave and that we were so very fortunate to experience it before it was discovered by the media." In this photograph, artist Nicholas Mirandon takes off on a left at Black's in 1965.

# Five

# NORTH COUNTY

Many rich surfing areas are found between Del Mar and Leucadia, including Solana Beach, Cardiff, and Encinitas, each boasting a bevy of break options and variety. Swami's, though it lacked the early lure and cosmopolitan charm of Windansea, took on a territorial imperative of its own. Here on Cardiff's main beach in 1952, San Diego County lifeguard John Elwell poses for a picture in his custom 1932 Ford Phaeton. A Bob Simmons board shares the back seat with a French Arbellet spear gun. John patrolled the beaches from Swami's to Seaside Reef. (Courtesy of John Elwell.)

Ed and Virginia Thomas of Escondido pose on the bluff at Torrey Pines in 1943. Ed's car was a 1936 Ford V-8 with three windows, highly polished chrome, and seven coats of lacquer. In order to get his board to the coast, Ed wrapped it in one of his mom's quilts and fastened it to the car's roof with lots of rope, as securely as possible. Even so, the couple checked the board repeatedly on the trip over and back. (Courtesy of Ed and Virginia Thomas.)

1940 - Ed and Virginia Thomas, Torrey Pines

Dave Woodall and Virginia Thomas stand with Ed's Pacific Systems "swastika model" board on the beach at Torrey Pines. Ed had the board for several years and surfed spots from Oceanside Pier to Mission Beach. The board weighed about 75 pounds and, at one time, had the small swastika emblem near the tail. Ed later chipped out the design in wood shop because of its offensive nature. (Courtesy of Ed and Virginia Thomas.)

Young Encinitas surfers proudly pose for a group photograph at Moonlight Beach in 1940. Pictured here are, from left to right, (first row) Jim Truax, Jimmy Groh, Ralph Swaim, and Ted Cozens; (second row) Hodie Zimmerman and Leonard "Buddie" Bunyard. Jim was one of the earliest serious surfers in the area and a mentor to many who followed. (Courtesy of SDHM.)

In this 1948 aerial view of Cardiff Beach, the Beacon Inn is at far left and George's Restaurant, which was run by the San Clemente family, is in the center. Old Highway 101 ran very close to the high tide line in those days and was often damaged by pounding winter storm surf.

Fred Ashley recalls: "It was in 1946, and I stacked those boards and staged that photograph so we would get a good picture of our Cardiff shack. We had just finished it off with the palm fronds, and were real proud of it. That board on the right, a hollow board, is buried about three feet in the sand—it was a huge board. The rest are balsa and redwood laminates. I made a little windjammer for the top. The river mouth is just off to the right of the shack." (Photograph by Evelyn Largent.)

Six friends enjoy a fresh-caught seafood cookout at the Cardiff shack in 1947. From left to right are John Largent, Bill Chilcoate, Angelo Rea, Evelyn Largent, Al Southworth (standing), Fred Ashley, and Don Briggs. Al was also an accomplished diver and later became the surfing coach at San Dieguito High School. (Courtesy of Evelyn Largent.)

Looking at ease on his homemade board, Jim Truax cruises the surf at Guayule in 1949. Guayule (pronounced why-oo-lee) was so named because the government had a crop of the rubber-producing plants growing on the land nearby. Production fizzled out when the need for domestically grown rubber waned with the war years, and the popular surf spot became known as Terramar. (Courtesy of SDHM.)

Jim Truax (left) and a young Phil Edwards are on an outing in Malibu in the early 1950s. Jim grew up right near Swami's and began surfing there in the late 1930s. His surfing and shaping skills made him the perfect mentor for many who followed in his footsteps. A lifelong educator and high school principal, Jim always understood the strong pull surfing had on students. (Courtesy of SDHM.)

Ron McCarver poses with his Velzy board on the beach in Cardiff in 1950. In this image, Ron wears a lava-lava, a sort of Hawaiian wrap for men. "We'd cruise the Goodwill store and look for tropical fabrics or trunks or shirts, because that's the style everybody wanted. Plus, we always wore Hawaiian clothes to the Windansea luaus." (Courtesy of Ron McCarver.)

Fred Ashley (left), wearing the sailor's hat, John Largent (center, in his signature straw hat, and Angelo Rea catch a long ride in the Cardiff surf in 1947. John, who graduated with honors from San Dieguito High School the previous year, was once suspended from school for bleaching his hair. (Courtesy of Fred Ashley.)

From left to right, Gary Vienna, Mike Kiefer, Fred Ashley, and Steve Mitchell hang out at the Del Mar Pleasure Pier in 1956. Mike did the artwork on his board. "All of our boards were homemade at this time, and some, of course, worked better than others in the water," says Fred. "Later on I bought a board that Billy Hamilton shaped at Surfboards Hawaii—that was one sweet board." (Courtesy of Fred Ashley.)

Fred Ashley steps on the running board of the county lifeguard service truck while on duty in Solana Beach in the mid-1950s. Improperly sporting an aloha shirt while on duty, Fred had just gotten out of submarine service for the U.S. Navy and was happy to return to lifeguarding at his old stomping grounds. (Courtesy of Fred Ashley.)

When there was no surf, some of the guys got to horsing around with a little game called "sand duning," which, basically, consisted of sliding down the built-up beach berms on their balsa surfboards. This batch of sand-duning contestants include, from left to right, Sam Sherman, John Hunt on the shoulders of Jun Chino, Fred Ashley, and Mike Kiefer. (Courtesy of Fred Ashley.)

Fred Ashley surfs Cardiff with some style in 1956, wearing the Outrigger trunks he brought back from a recent trip to Hawaii. Fred picked up some surfing tips from his good friend Rabbit Kekai while he was there. (Courtesy of Fred Ashley.)

Encinitas' Linda Benson, tired of watching her brother and his friends surf on their own boards, finally talked her father into buying her one of her own. Linda, at age 15, became the youngest contestant at the annual Makaha International and flew home to Lindbergh Field a champion. While on Oahu, Linda also braved 18-foot waves at Waimea Bay, the first woman to do so. (Photograph by LeRoy Grannis.)

In 1963, Linda was the first woman featured on the cover of a surf magazine. Despite these and other remarkable accomplishments, this talented and modest woman never really considered herself a professional athlete—she was just content to be a surfer. (Photograph by John Elwell.)

(1) Dru Harrison, Hermosa Beach, 1967 Junior Champion; (2) Peter Johnson, Oceanside; (3) Dick Moon, La Jolla; (4) Mike Tabeling, Cocoa Beach, Fla.; (5) Neal Norris, La Jolla; (6) Cheer Critchlow, Cardiff. (Photo by LeRoy Grannis)

The Junior Championships in Huntington Beach reflect the depth and ability of San Diego–area surfers at that time. Oceanside's Peter Johnson, third from left, was already a seasoned competitor, having been tested in Hawaiian waters years earlier as part of the Windansea contingency, and was on his way to international fame. (Courtesy of Glen McInery.)

Dale Woodward team riders Gary (left) and Billy Brummett pose with their trophies and beautiful boards in the backyard of their Cardiff home in 1965. Local board maker Woodward was also one of the most highly regarded boatbuilders on the West Coast and was one of the county's top fishermen. (Courtesy of Diana Brummett.)

County lifeguards pose for a group photograph at the Solana Beach station in 1960. The guards, pictured here from left to right, are (first row) Russell Staggs, Knox Harris, Dave Willingham, and Marsh Malcolm; (second row) Mike Considine, Peter Critchlow, John Bowen, John Hunt, Peter Zovanyi, Red Shade, Bill Hunt, and Capt. Jim Lathers. (Photograph by Tom Keck; courtesy of Marsh Malcolm.)

The Pleasure Pier in Del Mar was constructed around the early 20th century for the use of the guests at the Del Mar Hotel. Remington Jackson recalls: "Surfing was restricted to the south of the pier, and, for some reason, it was the best spot. The middle section later collapsed so the county got the UDT guys from the navy to blow the pilings out off the bottom. Great show for all the kids!" (Courtesy of DMHS.)

A clear photograph of Swami's, one of North County's most infamous reef breaks and top winter surfing spots, shows that the waves here were crowded even in the 1960s. It was named after the proximity to the lotus-towered Self Realization Fellowship community nearby. On the horizon, shades of the huge kelp beds offshore are visible. The kelp beds sometimes provide a natural barrier from the wind, and the series of reef fingers on the bottom makes for pristine waves with the best winter swells. (Photograph by LeRoy Grannis.)

A band of friends from Coronado takes a surf safari to Swami's in Encinitas in 1958. Jens Morrison reminisces: "All of us who ride waves are travelers and searchers—our eyes and ears are tuned in all the time—a sort of sixth sense. We know when the surf is big. We freeze our rear ends off during dawn patrol." Hardy surfers here include, from left to right, Roger Ryan, Doug Vann, Phil Thorpe, Tom Carlin, Steve Lindsay, Wendy Wagner, Roddy Spence, and Bob Moore. (Photograph by Tom Keck.)

94

Swami's was only occasionally surfed before World War II. Big days in winter could mean waves up to 10 or 12 feet marching in from the northwest, hairy, with a big, fast peak and a long wall to the inside. The locals pretty much had it good until the emerging surf media put the information out there for all to see.

Rusty Miller manages a tricky right at Swami's. He was able to enjoy the relatively peaceful anonymity of his local break before it was played up in the magazines. By 1965, the likeable Encinitas resident was the top-ranked surfer in America and one of the best big-wave riders in the world. Rusty and Mike Doyle also founded Surf Research and marketed the first commercially successful surf wax.

Malcolm McCassey, one of the founders of Swami's Surfing Society, catches a long right in 1964. An excellent surfer and stylish noserider, Malcolm was one of the young, talented set of regulars at Swami's that included Rusty Miller, Linda Benson, Mike Holodick, and Randy Miller. The shallow inside section of Swami's is still called "Malkie's Reef" by locals in the know, testament to his surfing prowess and dedication to the break he loved. (Photograph by LeRoy Grannis.)

Don Hansen, founder of one of the most successful and long-lived surfing establishments in North County, proudly displays his very first board—a Pat Curren balsa—at the old Swami's parking lot in 1958. Don often slept in his prized, blue 1955 Chevy panel truck. (Courtesy of Don Hansen.)

Randy Miller cross-steps on a small right at Swami's in the early 1960s. According to his good buddy Jens Morrison, Randy "was a wonderful guy, a good surfer, actually one of the best in Swami's Surfing Society—but we had to pick on him from time to time, all in good jest." (Courtesy of Diana Brummett.)

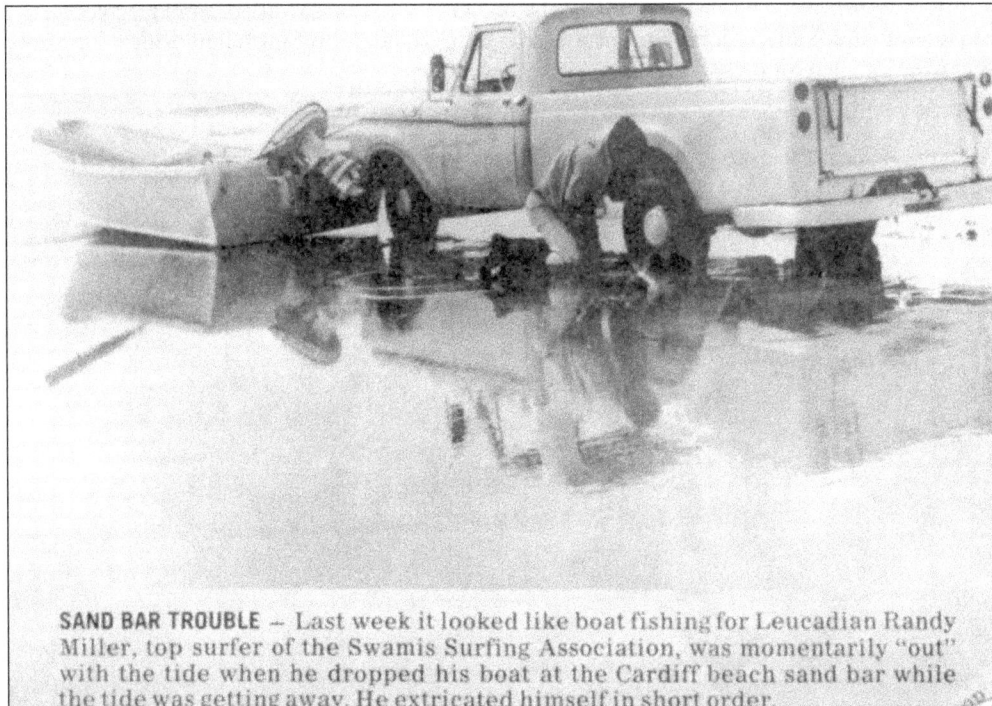

SAND BAR TROUBLE — Last week it looked like boat fishing for Leucadian Randy Miller, top surfer of the Swamis Surfing Association, was momentarily "out" with the tide when he dropped his boat at the Cardiff beach sand bar while the tide was getting away. He extricated himself in short order.

Randy Miller gets his truck and trailer stuck on a sand bar in Cardiff while trying to launch his boat at low tide. It was perfectly legal to drive cars on the beach and launch boats from any beach or bay at that time. (Courtesy of Glen McInery.)

In the mid-1960s, the reconstituted Swami's club was full of young talent. Contestants posing with their trophies after a contest at Moonlight Beach include, from left to right, (first row) Brad Bernard, Mark Rodriguez, Leroy Ley, and Danielle Corn; (second row) Cheer Critchlow, Kenny Bernard, Nicky Eaton, Eddie Eaton, Danny Erickson, Randy Miller, Carol Hagbloom, Sid Madden, Wally Wallace, John Cunnison, John Slingerland, John Smith, and Mike Cunnison. (Courtesy of Glen McInery.)

This classic shot of Encinitas local Cheer Critchlow was taken at the Pillbox in Solana Beach on a cold, offshore day in 1967. The image is the signature logo for Hansen Surfboards and is still recognized today. (Photograph by Tom Keck.)

Jens Morrison adjusts his sunglasses at Moonlight Beach in 1958. "I bought this Velzy 'pig' board in 1957 for $30," recalls Jens. "A lot of guys made their own boards, but I was lucky enough to buy a board now and then. Behind me is this great '57 Chevy pick-up that my grandfather, Popeye, bought for me from Harloff Chevrolet, and I pretty much cruised the coast from La Jolla to Trestles in it. Mike Dormer, an artist from La Jolla, did the bitchin' artwork on the board. I sure wish I had it today!" (Courtesy of Jens Morrison.)

Photographer John Hunt captured Jens Morrison in full trim on a fun day at Malkie's Reef. According to Jens, "The Encinitas area, at this time, was podunk rural—there was usually nothing happening, as opposed to Windansea, which had a more urban flavor and lent itself to more photograph documentation. Little did we know how we truly lived in a magical time for a while. By 1965, the halcyon days were gone—things went from pure, unassuming, rural paradise to the modern era, seemingly overnight." (Photograph by John Hunt.)

In the 1950s and 1960s, tandem surfing was a much anticipated contest event. Contestants were expected to show proficiency with a number of complex lifts and maneuvers. Locals Don Hansen and Danielle Corn practice their tandem surfing routines on the beach in Cardiff. The pair went on to compete professionally, and Danielle later teamed with Mike Doyle. (Courtesy of Glen McInery.)

Tandem surfing requires strength, balance, and cooperation between partners. Teams spent hours practicing, both in and out of the water. The women were selected for their smaller size and agility, and some were accomplished gymnasts. This photograph shows Gary Brummett and Danielle Corn practicing their lifts on waves at Cardiff. As a team, they competed in several amateur events. (Courtesy of Diana Brummett.)

Diana Brummett strikes a stretch-five pose on her Hansen board. Older brothers Billy, Gary, and Dennis would haul the family paddleboard to the beach in Cardiff before they were in their teens and became excellent surfers. Diana followed in their footsteps and carved a niche as one of the top female surfers in the area. (Photograph by Richard Dowdy.)

Ninth-grader Gary Brummett goes right at Swami's in the early 1960s. Gary purchased this board from his idol, Rusty Miller. Later, as a junior in high school, Gary earned enough class credits to leave the campus every day by 11:00 a.m. to head straight for the surf, making his classmates quite envious. (Courtesy of Diana Brummett.)

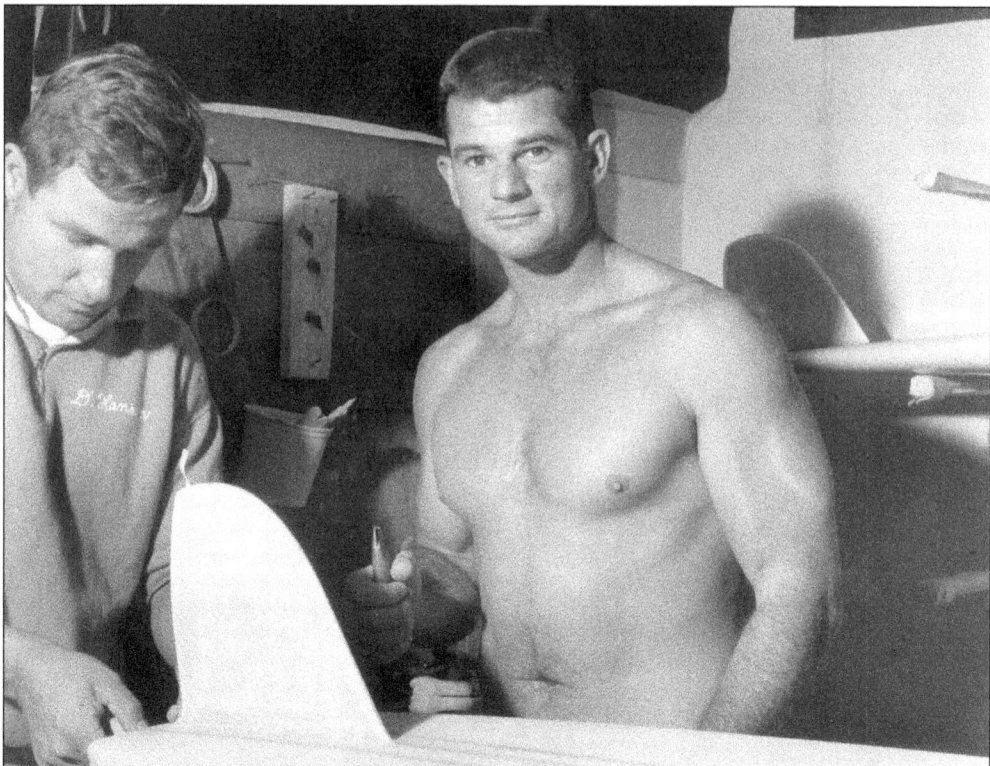

In 1963, Don Hansen (left) and Ron Smith confer in Don's shop on Coast Highway in Cardiff. Ron, a local surfer who produced surfboards with Don, was also an expert diver and U.S. Navy Seal. (Photograph by Tom Keck.)

John Bugley's face reflects in the wet gloss coat he is applying at Hansen's factory in Cardiff, 1964. Note the lack of any protective clothing or masks used for this chemical- and fume-filled activity. (Photograph by Richard Dowdy.)

Ryan Dotson, a La Jollan who moved to Hawaii to open Maui Surf Shop, came back to North County to work as a sander for Hansen. The sanding room was on a porch outside the factory barn. The railroad trestles over San Elijo Lagoon can be seen in the background. (Photograph by Richard Dowdy.)

Lounging on a pair of resin-filled barrels and comfortably oblivious to the potential fire hazard he is courting, Larry Templin takes a cigarette break in Hansen's shaping room. Unfortunately, some surfers found out how volatile the new, synthetic board-building materials were the hard way. (Photograph by Richard Dowdy.)

Larry Templin was checking the surf at Beacon (not Beacon's), seemingly unaware that buddy Eddie Eaton was sleeping one off in the stack of boards on the truck. (Photograph by Richard Dowdy.)

Ed Wright hangs five at Beacon in July 1963. Ed worked for John Price at Surfboards Hawaii in Leucadia, and John taught him the art of shaping. The instructions stuck, and Ed went on to establish Sunset Surfboards on old Highway 101 in Encinitas. Many of the next generation of Encinitas surfers earned their wings under Ed's tutelage. (Photograph by Richard Dowdy.)

Richard "Slick" Dowdy and Jim "J. J."
Jenks conceived the infamous Stone Steps
Invitational Surf Contest and Love-In one
late afternoon at Hansen's in Cardiff. Slick
and J. J. thought it was time for some surf,
fun, and beer at the beach. The inaugural
contest in 1967 was called the "33rd Annual"
to give a sense of history to the event.
Here winner Doug Erickson is pictured
with his 1967 trophy. (Photograph by
Richard Dowdy.)

Participants of the Stone Steps Invitational had to imbibe a resin bucketful of beer (about two
quarts) before their heats, and each heat won meant more beer had to be swilled. Competitors with
serious beer-drinking credentials dominated the list of annual winners. Butch Van Artsdalen (1968
winner), Mike Doyle, and Donald Takayama (multiple champion) all took home the prestigious
Sorrento Valley Yacht Club Perpetual Trophy. Frequent contestants included Dale Dobson, Owl
Chapman, Mike Purpus, George Draper, Dick Dale (Wipe-Out of the Day Award winner), Eddie
Eaton, John Price, Gary Stuber, and Gary Neves. (Photograph by Richard Dowdy.)

Photographer Tom Keck comments: "After I had taken the standard pose for the Del Mar Lifeguards' annual picture, I thought it would be fun to do a 'cheesecake' shot, if Joyce agreed. She [Joyce Hoffman] had just passed the rigorous testing and became the first female lifeguard in Del Mar." Del Mar lifeguards from 1971 are, from left to right, (supporting their female member) Tom Cozens, Robert Maurer, Robert Smith, Vernon Rye III, and Brad Smith; (standing) Dan Jago, Petey Hoff, Capt. Gardner Stevens, and Dave Grossman. (Photograph by Tom Keck.)

Mike Doyle rides the nose with his trademark casual style during the mid-1960s in Del Mar. He became a world champion surfer and is certainly one of the most easily recognized legends of today. Many of his memories of living in the North County area are captured in his autobiography, *Morning Glass*. Photographer LeRoy Grannis considers Mike to be *the* waterman of the second half of the last century. (Photograph by Tom Keck.)

# Six

# CARLSBAD AND OCEANSIDE

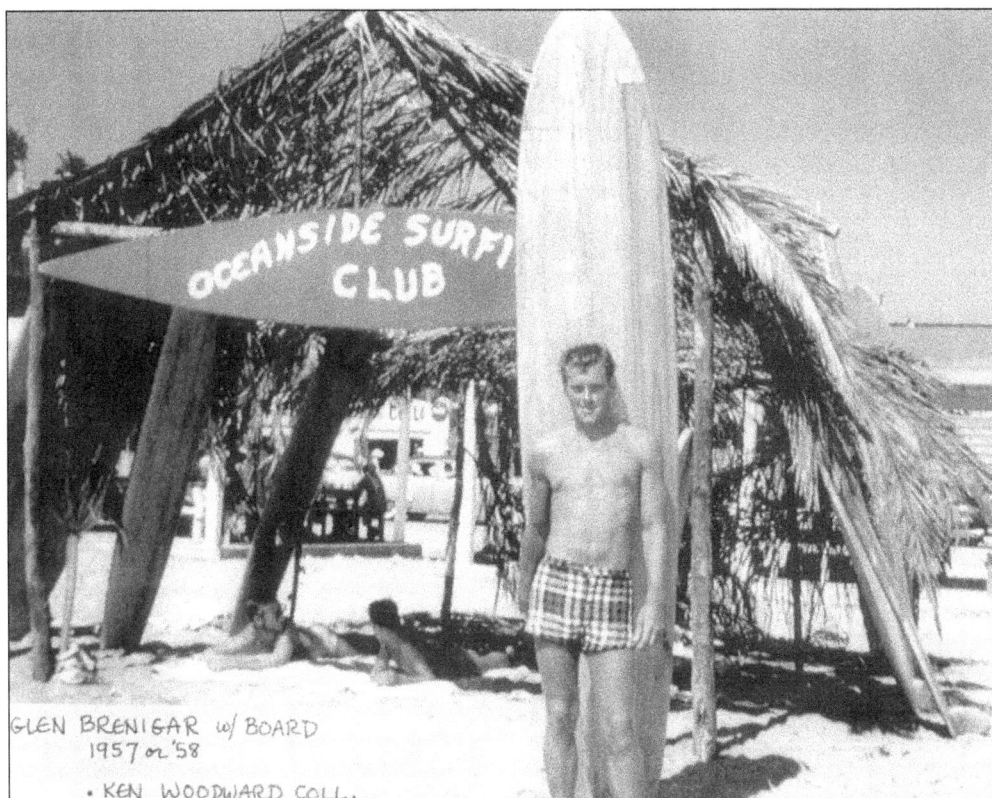

Many locals recall seeing surfboards in Carlsbad and Oceanside, from Ponto in south Carlsbad to Del Mar Jetties on Camp Pendleton, from the mid-1930s. This long stretch of beaches provides endless wave opportunities, and the Oceanside Pier has been a venue for a variety of world-class surfing competitions (board and bodysurfing) since the late 1950s. In this photograph, young Glen Brenigar stands with his balsa board in front of the Oceanside Surf Club Shack around 1957. The shack had been dismantled at Tamarack in Carlsbad and was reassembled near the pier for a summer beach party that was being planned. The local authorities quickly intervened, though, and the newly installed shack had to be taken down three days later. (Courtesy of Ken Woodward.)

Robert Stier relaxes on his paddleboard in the area known as "Tent City" on January 9, 1938. The beach was a haven for folks from the Los Angeles area looking to escape the crowds and congestion. Families would spend the entire summer here, and working fathers joined their broods on the weekends. (Courtesy of Robert Stier.)

Encinitas resident Jim Truax enjoyed the Carlsbad beaches regularly. Here he shoulders one of his homemade boards for a surf session at Guayule (now known as Terramar) in the mid-1940s. He spent many hours shaping boards for himself and others until surf shops began to dot the coast. (Courtesy of SDHM.)

Doug Tico poses with the pine and redwood surfboard he bought from George Miller for $65. When Doug started surfing, there were less than a dozen other surfers he knew of in Carlsbad and Oceanside. As he recalls, "I could drive my Ford Country Squire from Wisconsin Street all the way down to Seaside in south Cardiff—on the beach!" (Courtesy of John Oakley.)

Lifeguards and their young trainees pose near the Oceanside Pier during the early 1950s. Pictured here are, from left to right, (first row) Bill Maples, Reeves Smith, Phil Edwards, and Ted Tuck; (second row) Bruce Monroe, Byron Jessup, and John Oakley; (third row) Doug Tico, Dick Geyer, and Joe Trotter. (Courtesy of John Oakley.)

This is an early photograph of Frank Hecklinger's shop, Tamarack Surfboards, which was in Carlsbad in the early 1960s. A natural athlete and semipro baseball player, Frank discovered surfing a decade earlier and became fascinated with board design. He combined finely honed woodworking skills and intuitive design abilities with his love of the ocean to come up with a business called Boards by Heck. His shop was unique in that Frank added a line of diving and scuba gear as well.

Cramer Jackson takes his balsa board out for an early-morning surf at Oceanside. An Oceanside native and lifeguard, Cramer also invented and produced a surfing board game in the early 1980s. (Courtesy of Cramer Jackson.)

"The lifeguard tower was first built at the very end of Oceanside Pier as a surveillance point during World War II. Local women manned shifts during daylight hours, keeping their eyes open for enemy submarines and aircraft," remembers John Oakley. "Just a couple of years after it was constructed a huge winter storm broke the tower from the pier and it washed ashore at the river mouth. City officials had the tower re-installed at the foot of the pier, where it continued in use for many years." (Courtesy of John Oakley.)

Lifeguards assemble in 1957 for a group shot that includes, from left to right, (first row) Bob Lobo, Johnny Damian, Ricky Wykoff, John Penrod, and "Whitey"; (second row) Don Sammons, Jim Carroll, Frank Evans, Keith Groves, Tillman Eakes, and Cramer Jackson. Some years before, Bette Jo Hoskins was the first female lifeguard in Oceanside and was involved in several rescues. (Courtesy of Cramer Jackson.)

A selection of surfboards sits dry-docked in 1954. "Betty's Restaurant there in the background was the mecca for all us kids," recalls Dick James. "Boy, if you had enough money for a burger and malt at Betty's you were in Nirvana. Even though I lived in Carlsbad, I surfed a lot in Oceanside, because of the high school we were all buddies. If we could get a ride to Betty's, we spent all day there." (Courtesy of Dick James.)

Dick James (with striped towel) and others hang out in the lot at Betty's Restaurant on the beach in Oceanside. Lollie Taylor was a waitress at Betty's for about five years and would make bathing trunks for the guys if they brought her the yardage. Drapery fabric was one of the favored materials. (Courtesy of Dick James.)

Down at the north end of the strand was Tent City. Summer vacationers would set up tents and spend weeks camping on the beach. Working fathers joined their families on the weekends. Lollie Taylor recalls: "My parents rented a tent for us to stay in while they were building a house in south Oceanside. We were fine until the river flooded and we lost a lot of stuff."

Summer residents of Tent City enjoyed hanging out and surfing in Oceanside, often returning year after year. Rock-and-roll music blared from newly popular transistor radios, and families flooded the sand on sunny days and holidays like the Fourth of July and Labor Day.

Dick James (left) and Jack "Murph the Surf" Murphy stand in front of Dick's house in 1954. "Jack lived a few doors down from me and we were both water people—did a lot of diving together, and he learned to surf on my board," says Dick. "Some time later Murphy and two others pulled the biggest jewel heist of the century when they robbed the American Museum of Natural History in New York City of 24 choice stones." (Courtesy of Dick James.)

Dick James ties his balsa Phil board atop his 1957 Volkswagen. "We sometimes went to Trestles, but that was a clandestine operation that had to be well thought out because the Marines could take your boards and gear and otherwise hassle you," recalls Dick. (Courtesy of Dick James.)

"Bill Draper [left] and I are at the south side of the pier in February, 1956," recalls Dick James. "The water was in the 50s, we didn't know what a wet suit or a leash was in those days. . . . The guy that took this picture deserves a lot of credit—he used a great big old box-type camera on a tripod—his name was Bucky Kettner." (Courtesy of Dick James.)

Dick James goes left at Tamarack in 1964. He remembers as though it were yesterday: "We were moderately concerned with fashion in those days. You could shop for stuff at the local Goodwill, but you had to go up to Laguna to get decent trunks, long ones that had a little pocket for the wax. Hawaiian style was favored. Because we were in our teens it was important to look good, to 'put on the dog,' so to speak." (Courtesy of Dick James.)

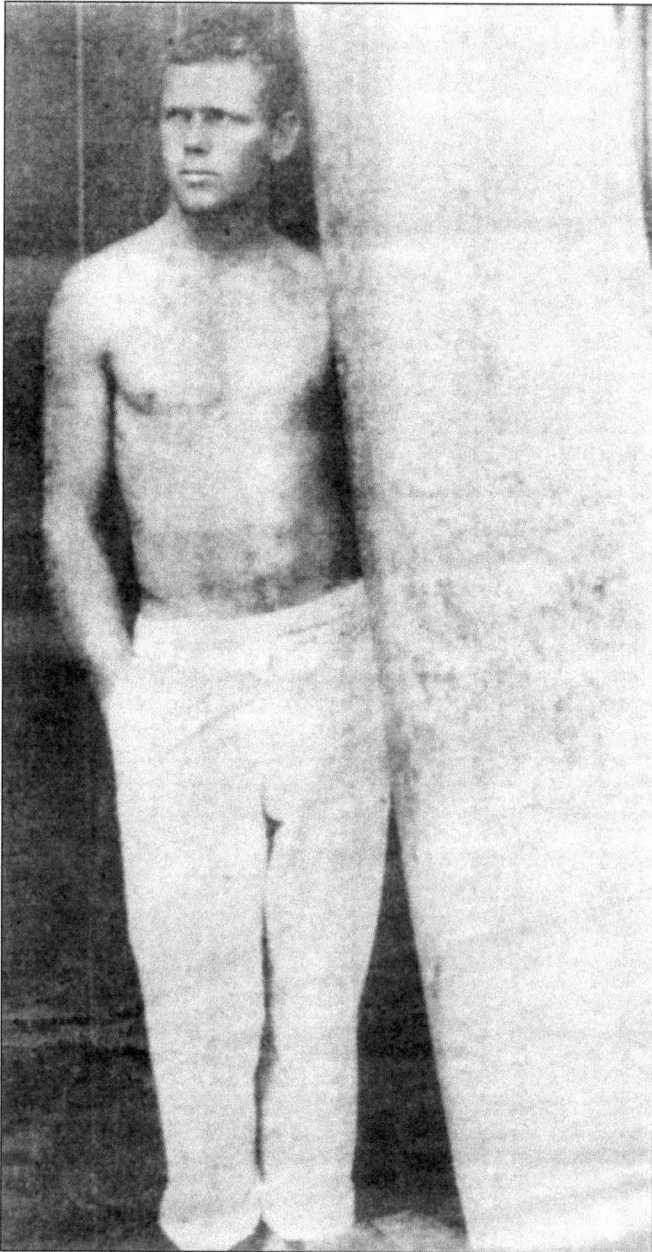

Phil Edwards had seen surfers in Long Beach as a youngster. When his family moved to Oceanside in 1946, he first tried surfing on a lifeguard paddleboard, and it did not take Phil long to realize it would be better if he had a fin and a smaller board. At San Onofre, Phil learned about balsa and fiberglass boards and began copying the progressive style of Mickey Dora. But Phil soon discovered that his innate ability, size, and power led to a style of his own, and he quickly became the finest surfer of his era. He took surfing to a level few could reach, though many tried to copy. "In the late 1950s, Phil would sail his Hobie [catamaran] from Oceanside to Swami's, and carried his board on the cat," recalls Jens Morrison. "Burned in my brain are the rides I saw him rip on a 10-foot gnarly wave—we would just come in from the water to watch him do his thing. His size gave him advantage and power to make moves that made him the best of the best, by far."

116

Phil Edwards pauses in front of a quiver of balsas in 1956. Says Dick James: "It probably took Phil about a day to shape a balsa. He'd have to glue about four 4 by 4s together, draw a pattern or use a template, then he'd jump up on top of the wood that was set over two sawhorses and started cutting away with a handsaw. Then he'd use a drawknife and start whaling away at it until he got the shape he was after." (Courtesy of Ken Woodward.)

Phil Edwards speeds into a cutback turn on a small, glassy day at Oceanside in 1965. Phil's surfing and shaping prowess were unmatched in his era, and his legendary surfboards remain some of the most valuable and sought-after shapes in existence. (Photograph by LeRoy Grannis.)

Winners of the 1958 Annual Paddleboard Contest in Oceanside display their hardware. Notable contestants include Tommy Zahn (standing center), who won the open division; L. J. Richards (kneeling left), winner of the 18-and-over resident division; and Don Sammons (kneeling right), who took top honor in the military division. Also pictured are Robert McEwen (standing left) and Bing Boca (standing right). (Courtesy of L. J. Richards.)

Winners pose with their trophies after a contest held at Tamarack in the mid-1960s. From left to right are Joyce Hoffman, David Nuuhiwa, Danielle Corn, Corky Carroll, and Rusty Miller. (Courtesy of Glen McInery.)

Born in Oceanside in 1939, Little John "L. J." Richards began surfing at age 14 on a balsa board that Phil Edwards had reshaped for him. Seen here on a break from lifeguard duties, L. J. heads to the nose on a different Phil board at Tamarack in 1957. This image is a still shot from Bill Stromberg's film *Hot Dog on a Stick*. (Courtesy of L. J. Richards.)

Glen Brenigar (left) and L. J. Richards attempt to shake hands while riding an overhead wave on their balsa boards at the south side of Oceanside Pier. One of the most enduring surfers and gentlemen, L. J. has many career highlights, including winning the U.S. Men's Surfing Championship at Huntington Beach in 1963 and receiving the LeRoy Grannis Waterman Award in 1990. (Courtesy of L. J. Richards.)

LeRoy Grannis was one of the first photographers to consistently document surfing, following in the footsteps of his friend and mentor "Doc" Ball. Known for his well-composed photograph images, LeRoy was a cofounder of *International Surfing* magazine (now *Surfing*) in 1964. A Hermosa Beach pioneer, "Granny," as he is known to friends, relocated to Carlsbad in the 1960s and surfed Tamarack every day for years. (Courtesy of LeRoy Grannis.)

Many people don't know that Tom Morey invented and sold boogie boards out of his garage in Carlsbad in the early 1970s. Local surfers remember that boogies came in a kit and had to be glued together. Says Tom: "Here's me, *c.* 1974, modeling my new pants product. I was dabbling into the clothing business. And with the paddleboard we'd also just come out with, the ULTRA. This shot was taken, probably by Bobby Szabad, on the beach in Carlsbad." (Courtesy of Tom Morey.)

Donald Takayama, founder of Hawaiian Pro Designs in Oceanside, first flew from Hawaii to shape for Dale Velzy when Donald was just 11 years old. A phenomenal surfer and shaper, he has influenced surfing for decades and has been designing signature model boards for top surfers since the 1960s.

WARNING
NO SWIMMING
OR SURFING

Surfers have, over the years, been subjected to shrinking playgrounds and increased regulations governing the use of ocean beaches and waves. At the Oceanside Pier, a warning sign seems to indicate that neither swimming nor surfing is allowed, but the faded last line reads "within 100 feet of the pier." (Photograph by Richard Dowdy.)

This historic photograph shows Beebe's drugstore on Hill Street and Third Street in Oceanside. Because of the store's proximity to the pier and excellent visibility, the city offered to lease the building to CSM in 1997.

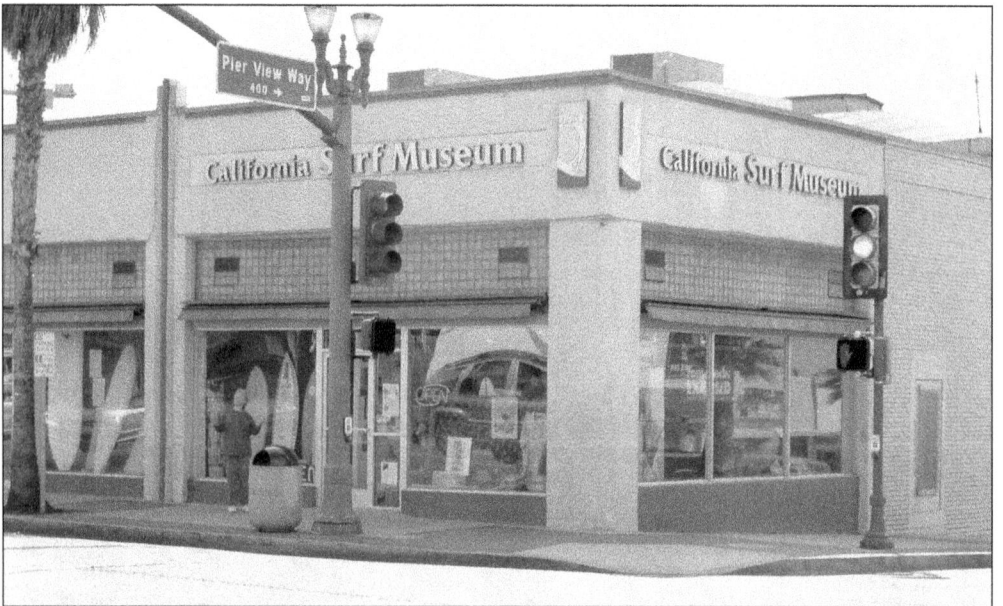

The California Surf Museum's current location is the corner of Coast Highway and Pier View Way, where, thanks to the City of Oceanside, it has hosted 20,000 visitors annually since 1997. CSM is open seven days a week, and admission is free! (Photograph by Tara Lee Torburn.)

## Seven

# SAN ONOFRE

San Onofre is a noble stretch of beach where many San Diego (and Los Angeles) surfers were able to hone their skills, test newfangled surfboard designs, and bask in the Hawaiian-influenced surf culture. Located in the northernmost reaches of San Diego County, San Onofre has been a gathering place for generations of Southern Californian surfers since the early 1930s, and today San O' is an internationally recognized mainland mecca for the family-oriented beach lifestyle. As such, San Onofre deserves an entire book of its own: The list of watermen who have frequented its generous breaks reads like a who's who of surfing. This scene, taken around 1950 by an unknown photographer, shows an impressive array of classic wood planks. San O' regular Bob Simmons (seated, wearing a hat) holds court with interested onlookers. Such moments represent a true turning point in modern surfboard development. (Photograph by Beni Reinhold; courtesy of Don Craig.)

Because of the original Pacific Coast Highway's proximity to the ocean, San Onofre had become one of the most popular surf spots in the county by the late 1920s. Swells fill into the massive reef break during both summers and winters, and rideable waves break at high and low tides. In 1936, a "fish camp" was established and soon was welcoming the small bands of surfers that came from up and down the coast. (Courtesy of Don Craig.)

The San Onofre Beach Camp parking pass was printed in a different color each year to discourage duplication, but it always featured the same photograph of George "Nellie Bly" Brignell in the center. This pass is the 1946 edition. (Courtesy of Bill Hein.)

Hammerhead's surf truck stands as backdrop for four San O' regulars in 1949. From left to right are Nils "Viking" Jensen, Robert "Hammerhead" Gravage, Edward "Pop" Proctor, and Ocean Beach's Bob Card. By this time, Pop had already become one of the beach's legendary figures, and decades later, he was considered to be the world's oldest surfer when he died in 1981 at age 99. A traditional memorial paddleout was held at San Onofre in his honor. (Photograph by Beni Reinhold.)

Following World War II, returning servicemen and their families were happy to rediscover this unique playground and flocked to the beach in droves, especially during the summer months. Because the beach and its access were leased from the military, it took regular and diplomatic communication between surfers and the commanding officers to maintain the delicate balance. One of San Onofre's most distinguished voices on behalf of the surfers was Dr. Barney Wilkes, seen at far right playing the guitar. (Photograph by Joe Quigg; courtesy of Beni Reinhold.)

This photograph shows the contestants of the 1939 Pacific Coast Championships at San Onofre. From left to right are surfers Tulie Clark, Al Bixeler, Don Okey, Bob "Half-Hour" Humphreys, Doc Paskowitz, Lloyd Baker (facing camera), Pete Peterson (seated), Gard Chapin, Vincent "Klotz" Lindberg, and Lorrin "Whitey" Harrison, the winner. Whitey is holding the Tom Blake trophy, and his name was subsequently inscribed on its plate along with the winners from 1928 to 1941 (the last year the contest was held).

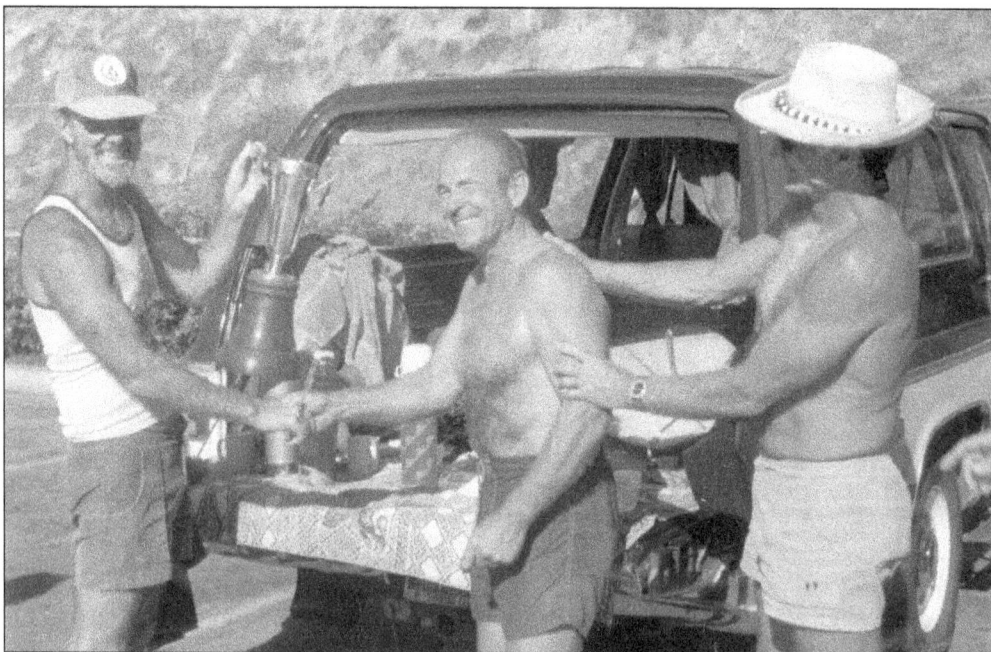

About 50 years after the 1939 photograph above, John Blankenship pretends to award the Tom Blake trophy to ruggedly fit Bud Caldwell, while Skeeter Malcolm eggs them on. The three San Diego–area surfing buddies often made the trip to San Onofre for the day, or weekend, and had been doing so since the 1940s. (Courtesy of Marsh Malcolm.)

The inscription on this 1972 photograph reads, "To Dick from Doug." Doug Craig, for many years one of the leading figures of the San Onofre Surfing Club, had sent his heartfelt regards to Pres. Richard M. Nixon after Nixon had the military turn over the lease to San Onofre Beach to the state park system. Up until that point, the club had been able to lease the beach from the hierarchy at Camp Pendleton for $1 per year. (Courtesy of Don Craig.)

George Boskoff shows good form as he retreats to the privacy of his car to change clothes following a surf session at Old Man's in 1939. It is simply our way of saying "The End."

Visit us at
arcadiapublishing.com

www.ingramcontent.com/pod-product-compliance
Lightning Source LLC
Chambersburg PA
CBHW050600110426
42813CB00008B/2409